W9-BUH-546

Mary for All Christians

Mary for All Christians

John Macquarrie

William B. Eerdmans Publishing Company
Grand Rapids, Michigan

Copyright © 1990 by John Macquarrie

First published in Great Britain in 1990 by Collins Religious Division
part of the Collins Publishing Group
8 Grafton Street, London W1X 3LA

This edition published 1991
by special arrangement with the
Collins Publishing Group by
William B. Eerdmans Publishing Co.
255 Jefferson Ave. S.E., Grand Rapids, Michigan 49503

All rights reserved. No part of this publication may be reproduced,
stored in a retrieval system, or transmitted—in any form or by any means,
electronic, mechanical, photocopying, recording, or otherwise—without prior
permission from the publisher.

Printed in the United States of America

Library of Congress Cataloging-in-Publication Data

Macquarrie, John.
Mary for all Christians / John Macquarrie.
p.   cm.
ISBN 0-8028-0543-4 (pbk.)
1. Mary, Blessed Virgin, Saint — Theology.   2. Mary, Blessed Virgin,
Saint, and Christian union.   I. Title.
BT613.M286   1991
232.91 — dc20   90-27067
                                                                    CIP

Contents

Foreword

In 1970 John Macquarrie came home from eight years as Professor of Systematic Theology at Union Theological Seminary, New York, after lecturing at his own university, Glasgow. He had of course been home before that, at such moments as for the 1968 Lambeth Conference, where (as again in 1978) he was a consultant. In Michaelmas 1970 he became a Canon of Christ Church and Oxford's Lady Margaret Professor of Divinity.

He was at the time working on three books, all published in 1972: *Existentialism, Paths in Spirituality* and *The Faith of the People of God*. None of his major writings so far has been mariological, i.e. not directly so. However he did in 1970 join the then quickly flourishing Ecumenical Society of the Blessed Virgin Mary (ESBVM), led at the time by its energetic — not to say frenetic — founder, Martin Gillett (d. 1980). He was soon called to participate at a depth fitting to his office and canonry. At the Society's Third International Ecumenical Congress, held at Birmingham in Easter Week 1975, he spoke upon 'God and the Feminine', beginning with the new liberation of women to greater freedom and dignity in society.

Professor Macquarrie showed that hitherto the Church has seemingly been hostile to this: Eve, subordinate to Adam, was made the proximate cause of the Fall; God is firmly masculine and generator of a Son; and St Paul seems to rank women second in mankind. In fact Christianity was instrumental in raising the status of women in society: while sociologically it may have reflected the *mores* of the secular state, theologically it became revolutionary. Even then cultural habit dies hard, and the weight of Hebrew monotheism, reacting against ancient fertility cults, remained doggedly masculine: the one amelioration has been the exalted role assigned to Mary in the New Testament. Gender and sexuality enter deeply into the psychology and personality of man, physical differences being so fundamental as to give rise to deep mental, personal and spiritual differences. Admittedly some of these come from centuries of cultural conditioning; and when a war occurs, women are found to have the resources to take on men's work. But no new fashion can disguise the fact that intellectual and emotional differences remain.

Professor Macquarrie has often since addressed the Society nationally, in London, or in one of the branches such as in Oxford; and chapters in this book are the polished revisions of what began perhaps as an evening in Pusey House or a contribution to a day conference elsewhere. He has listened as much as he has lectured, offering subsequent opinions that generated further reflection: and so in him there has grown up a sense of Mary's place in the divine economy which we see set forth in these pages.

Mary has traditionally been regarded as a sign of separation, not to say a bone of contention. It is enough to turn to a most eirenic source, the Final Report of ARCIC I (1982), to discover just how perennially this has been so. Concerning the two Marian definitions, the Immaculate Conception (1854) and the Assumption (1950), the joint Anglican and Roman Catholic signatories had this to say:

> Anglicans and Roman Catholics can agree in much of the truth that these two dogmas are designed to affirm. We agree that there can be but one mediator . . . We agree in recognizing the Christian understanding of Mary . . . We further agree in recognizing in Mary a model of holiness . . . We accept that it is possible to regard her as a prophetic figure . . . Nevertheless the [two] dogmas raise

a special problem for those Anglicans who do not consider that the precise definitions given by these two dogmas are sufficiently supported by Scripture. For many Anglicans the teaching authority of the Bishop of Rome, independent of a Council, is not recommended by the fact that through it these Marian doctrines were proclaimed as dogmas binding on all the faithful. Anglicans would also ask whether, in any future union between our two Churches, they would be required to subscribe to any such dogmatic statements. One consequence of our separation has been a tendency for Anglicans and Roman Catholics alike to exaggerate the importance of the Marian dogmas in themselves at the expense of other truths more closely related to the foundation of the Christian faith.

This non-agreeing statement clearly shows the dilemma; and it should be remarked that this very passage appears in full at the outset of the Society's main collection of occasional papers, *Mary's Place in Christian Dialogue* (St Paul Publications 1982), with the observation that the above acceptances followed by the caveats 'are all rounded out in some measure in the papers that follow below: there it may be seen how the Marian definitions emerged and how soundly based they are in biblical theology'. And that has since its foundation been the task of the ESBVM. Its existence has been 'to promote ecumenical devotion and the study, at various levels, of the place of the Blessed Virgin Mary in the Church, under Christ'. Mary covers the human predicament from conception to coronation, from sin to salvation, from carnality to the Cross. She is the *Mater Ecclesiae*, as Paul VI proclaimed her during the Second Vatican Council. She is the God-bearer, *Theotokos*, as the earliest Councils proclaimed her. She proclaimed herself 'handmaid of the Lord'.

The society was born as an idea in Brussels in 1966 during celebrations of the fortieth anniversary of the completion of the Malines Conversations (1921–6), unofficial talks in depth between church leaders Anglican and Catholic. Cardinal Léon-Josef Suenens (successor of Cardinal Mercier of Malines) and Bishop Allison of Winchester both encouraged the founder, the Catholic convert Martin Gillett, to turn such a problem as mariology 'from a cross to a joy'. In 1967 the first official meeting was called in London; and in the next couple of years, by some grace known only to God, the ESBVM prospered at a rate of growth and acceptance quite unexpected. From the earliest days, such leading figures as the Anglican Bishop Eric Kemp, the Methodist Dr Gordon Wakefield and the Roman Catholic Bishop Mervyn Alexander have given their services as co-chairmen. The Methodist Dr John Newton, the Anglican Bishop Graham Leonard and the Orthodox Bishop Kallistos Ware have acted as patrons. When Abbot Basil became Cardinal Hume, he took on the presidency (1976); and when Bishop Robert Runcie became Cantuar (1980), he asked to be co-president. Support comes from a dozen branches, as far afield as Washington and Rome; and from many other souls whose expertise is the love of Mary and love of fellow Christians, with a vast urge to intermingle the two.

Part of our glory, it must be said, is the sequence of International Congresses. During the last decade they were held during Easter Week or late summer alternately in Canterbury (1981), Dublin (1984), Chichester (1986) and Liverpool (1989) — and at the last we had liturgical and devotional recourse to not one but three cathedrals! The Congresses issue in Proceedings of book length. For the 1980s they were respectively these: *Mary and Ecumenism (The Way* supplement 45), *Mary in Christian Tradition (The Way* supplement 51), *Mary and the Churches* (Columba Press), *Mary in Doctrine and Devotion* (Columba Press). And as well, each Newsletter — three a year — carries with it a pamphlet putting to print the best current lecture/

meditation/dialogue in the Society's activities — and some of the author's chapters herein have first seen the light in that mode. We have been blessed by all our members, not least Oxford's former Lady Margaret Professor.

Alberic Stacpoole, OSB
Solemnity of Mary, the Mother of God,
1 January 1990

Author's Preface

This is a book about Mary, the Mother of Jesus Christ. In the past, such a book might have been controversial, for Christians in different traditions have taken very different attitudes toward Mary. Some have esteemed her highly, others have virtually ignored her. But the ecumenical spirit of recent years has been encouraging Christians to try to understand and appreciate one another's traditions better, so this book is 'for all Christians' and is written in the hope that they may find in Mary resources for reconciliation rather than conflict.

Most of the chapters of this book (with the exception of Chapter 4, which was an Assumption Day Lecture given at Walsingham Parish Church) began as papers for the Ecumenical Society of the Blessed Virgin Mary. This society is a sign of the new times, for its membership is made up of Roman Catholics, Orthodox, Anglicans, Lutherans, Methodists, Reformed and others.

At the end of the book, I have included an 'Ecumenical Office', developed by the Society for use by individuals and groups who wish to bring Mary more directly into their devotions, in the hope of making this valuable resource more widely available. Further copies may, of course, be obtained from the Society.

I wish to express thanks to the Revd Dom Alberic Stacpoole, OSB, who encouraged me to write the book, Mrs Jill Pinnock who helped in many ways, and the publishers, especially Mr Stratford Caldecott.

Part One

1   *God and the Feminine*

Of the many far-reaching social changes that have been taking place in recent years, one of the most important is the so-called 'sexual revolution'. In the whole field of sexual relations and conduct, there has been a major shift in values. What was once forbidden has become acceptable, and what was once acceptable is so no longer. No doubt some aspects of the sexual revolution have been very questionable, perhaps even disastrous, but there have also been important gains. Chief among these is the movement toward greater equality of the sexes, which means in effect more freedom and dignity for women.

This aspect of the sexual revolution is one that must commend itself to Christians, for it accords with the Christian teaching that all human beings have value for God. But the enhanced status of women has not been brought about explicitly by Christian teaching, but by the profound economic, political, intellectual and social changes that have been going on in the western world for about two hundred and fifty years, and seem likely to spread across the whole planet. So theologians must in the new situation think again about the Church's teaching on sexuality in general, and about the place of women in particular. As I have indicated, the sexual revolution is an ambiguous phenomenon, and it may be that Christianity has some wisdom to contribute that will help to ensure that the revolution has a healthy outcome.

But the trouble is that Christianity too seems to be ambiguous on these questions. There are contradictory interpretations of the influence which the Church has exerted in the past on the place of women in society.

Though I have said that equality of the sexes is something that must commend itself to all Christians, this is not obvious from the record. There are contradictory interpretations of the influence of Christian teaching on these matters in the past. Today one often hears expressed the opinion that Christian teaching and practice have been hostile to the cause of greater freedom and dignity for women. Thus, in the creation story, the woman is subordinate to the man, and is the proximate cause of his fall into sin; in the picture of society presented in the Old Testament, men predominate, though certainly women also take part and have an important influence on the course of events, and on the formation of the people of Israel and of individuals within it; above all, the teaching about God in the Old Testament represents him in terms that give a strongly masculine impression — the typical images show him as King, Judge, a mighty Warrior. The New Testament does not seem to bring much change in these matters. When God reaches out in his love toward the human race, the story which expounds this love is that of a Father sending his only Son; the new people of God, the Church, emerges as a male-dominated society, even if it is sometimes represented as a bride. Paul, probably the person who above all others had the decisive voice in forming the thinking of the new people of God, has often been considered — though it may be unjustly — as something of a misogynist, determined to allow to women only a second-class citizenship in the people of God.

But, of course, that is only one possible interpretation of the impact of Christianity on the status of women. On the other side, one finds the view that, in rejecting paganism with its goddesses, priestesses and fertility cults, the ethical monotheism of the Old Testament made possible a new sexual morality which ruled out any tendency to regard women as merely or primarily sex-objects; that Jesus numbered women among his disciples and clearly valued them very highly, so much so that the tradition tells us that he made one of them the first witness to his resurrection; that Paul, in spite of what he had said elsewhere, teaches that in Christ the difference between male and female, like the differences between social classes and ethnic groups, is of no account. Those who would draw attention to these other aspects of the Christian record would, of course, admit that the Church has not in fact lived up to the insights to which it has claimed to give allegiance. But they would claim that authentic Christian teaching, if it is allowed free expression and is put into practice, is favourable to the cause of women, and in spite of all the lapses that there have been, has in fact been favourable on the whole.

In mentioning those aspects of Christianity which have been beneficial to women, I omitted one of the most important of all because, since it is to be the main topic of this book, it calls for a special mention. I mean, the place of the Blessed Virgin Mary. That place is indispensable in the New Testament scheme of salvation. The Bible starts off with an unfavourable picture of woman, as that member of the human couple who first yielded to the temptation to sin. But the New Testament compensates for this by giving to Mary a part in the drama of salvation — a part which I have not hesitated to call 'indispensable'. From a very early date in the history of the Church, Mary was being honoured for her part in salvation, and inevitably the honour paid to her reflected on women in general. If in the Genesis story of the first couple, Eve is put into the shade by Adam, in the gospel story of the new creation in Christ, the pre-eminence belongs to Mary above Joseph. Moreover, the fact that

Mary was believed to be a virgin implied that women can have dignity simply as human persons, and independent of the roles of wife or mother. Though these remarks suggest that the position accorded to Mary has been helpful to the image of women in general, this is a matter of dispute. Once again, conflicting views have arisen, and we shall find such conflicts recurring again and again as we study the themes of mariology. Thus, Protestant theologians who have been willing to acknowledge that a special respect is due to Mary have usually held that she derives this entirely from her relation to her Son, Jesus. She has no independent worth beyond that which belongs to any human being, and her special position, if it is conceded that she has one, arises solely from her role as mother of Jesus. As against this, some radical feminist theologians desire to stress Mary's independence. They lay stress on the tradition of her perpetual virginity, which they interpret as a symbol of female autonomy. So at this point the traditional teaching about Mary is caught in a crossfire between Protestant critics who fear that she might be given a status that obscures her subordination to Christ, and feminist critics who claim that in her own right Mary introduces a feminine element into the work of salvation. Some very difficult and controversial questions open up at this point. Is the work of salvation something that is carried out by God alone, with human beings (including Mary) as no more than passive instruments in his hands? This principle of *sola gratia,* 'by grace alone', was fundamental to the Reformation and any erosion of it would still be resisted by the evangelical and reformed churches. But the alternative view, that some human co-operation or synergism with God is required in the work of salvation, has been gaining strength in modern times, and is a matter which we shall have to consider later. Some Catholic writers have given to Mary the title of *Corredemptrix,* which does seem to imply her active co-working in the saving events at the centre of Christianity. In a sense, this co-operation of Mary symbolizes the co-operation of humanity, but the fact that it is here located in a woman can hardly fail to raise the image of womanhood to a new level.

One reason for the many conflicts in the field of mariology is the co-existence in Christian teaching of both sociological and theological factors, and these are never more than partially reconciled. Sociologically, a religious institution tends to reflect the traditional *mores* and so it usually exercises a conservative influence. Theologically, however, such an institution may be bringing in new and even revolutionary ideas, without being at the time fully aware of the implications of these ideas. One could even say — if the comparison may be allowed — that the theology is like a time-bomb which will explode at some future date with unforeseeable consequences. Thus it could be argued that Paul's apparently negative attitudes to women and his insistence that they should stay in the background reflect the social conditions of his time, and perhaps Christian women had no other way of living as Christians or following in the way of Jesus Christ. But Paul's own bold theological utterances about the end of discrimination in Christ were already contradicting the system to which he was accustomed and which he accepted as a matter of course, presumably without realizing the full extent of the challenge which his own theology was offering to his society.

But even if we were to acknowledge the force of such an argument in the case of Paul, deep underlying problems remain. We could say that the main problem is this: the Judaeo-Christian tradition, both in theology and practice, has had a predominantly masculine orientation. As a result, it has at least given the impression that it considers women to be further removed from God than men, and thus denies them a full humanity. We have, of course, already noted that Hebrew monotheism could reach its sublime moral conceptions only through its unremitting struggle with the Canaanite fertility religions. In these pagan cults, both gods and goddesses were recognized, and sexual intercourse was incorporated into the religious rituals. Certainly, such a state of affairs did not bring dignity to women or to men either, and did not promote any truly human understanding of love, sexuality and marriage. Perhaps the new prophetic and ethical religion of the Hebrews could only attain its full stature through the rigorous exclusion of goddesses and priestesses, and perhaps this was the way along which one would eventually arrive at a better appreciation of sexuality and a higher place for women in society, as has in fact happened in the Judaism which is heir to the religion of the Old Testament. Perhaps, too, religious reformations can take place only through exaggerated and onesided changes, so that at a later stage corrections have to be introduced. Protestants are still correcting some of the extravagances of the sixteenth century, and are even in some cases (such as mariology!) trying to restrain reforming zealots among Roman Catholics from embarking on a repetition of the old Protestant excesses.

In any case, much has happened since the now distant days of the Hebrew prophets, and I think both their Jewish and their Christian spiritual descendants have become aware that some elements in their heritage need to be re-examined. As far as Christians are concerned, there lie between us and the Old Testament not only Jesus Christ but the Virgin Mary, both as she is presented in the New Testament and in the subsequent development of the tradition. When some rethinking is required in Christian faith and practice — and is there ever a time when rethinking is not demanded? — the first move should be to look again at the tradition. Can we find there elements, perhaps hitherto neglected or not rightly appreciated? Can we find in such elements the resources needed for new problems, rather than in radical innovations which are not truly rooted in the Christian revelation? Confronted as we are today by a strong sense of dissatisfaction among many women about the place which the Church accords to them both in faith and practice, is it to a renewed understanding of and devotion to the Blessed Virgin that we must look for a solution to some of the problems?

If one does decide to look in this direction, then first of all it will be necessary to overcome some quite powerful prejudices that stand in the way. These embody different and sometimes opposing points of view. On the one side, there are theologians who suspect that any desire to honour Mary or to give her a more prominent place in theology may lead us back to the paganism against which the Hebrew prophets struggled in their day. Such theologians point to some of the more exaggerated devotions that have been paid to Mary and see in them a survival into Christianity of the old Mediterranean cult of the *Magna Mater*. They can also point to the emergence in extreme feminist groups of 'goddess worship' in explicitly non-Christian forms. But while some pagan features have in fact clung to some of the devotions offered to Mary and while it is also true that some women have reacted so strongly against Christianity that they have attempted to revive goddess cults, these are not points that should be given an exaggerated importance. Mary's place within the structure of Christianity has a sound theological basis and is independent of any pagan cult of the feminine. Of course, if there was some spiritual or metaphysical justification for such a cult (a point we shall have to consider), then perhaps this is accommodated in Christian attitudes to Mary. But her place in Christianity must be secured on a theological basis. It cannot be secured by an appeal to pre-Christian and pre-Israelite practices, though even less can it be rejected as basically a survival from such origins.

Still another prejudice against Mary arises from a different point of view. Many women in the Church have come to believe that the veneration accorded to Mary has been a subtle means of inculcating in women generally the acceptance of an inferior role. Mary is represented as meek, obedient, self-effacing, and this, it is said, has projected an ideal for women designed to keep them in subjection. But is there not a serious misunderstanding here? Humility is a Christian virtue not confined to Mary and not recommended only to women. Christ was also meek and humble. Indeed, one might say that this is the very heart of the revelation of God in Christ. God has come among us in meekness and humility, not in power and overwhelmingness. The message is hammered home repeatedly. Christ emptied himself and humbled himself (Phil. 2:7–8); he came not to be served but to serve (Mk. 10:45); he washed the feet of his disciples (Jn. 13:5); when he was reviled, he did not revile in return (1 Pet. 2:23). Humility is an ideal for all Christians, not just for women. Certainly, the vocation of the Christian is not to be a doormat — that would sometimes be the very opposite of a truly loving service. But it is just as certain that the Christian should never use religion for self-assertion. We live in a time when confrontation and abrasiveness seem to be counted as virtues. But Christian love 'is patient and kind; love is not jealous or boastful; it is not arrogant or rude. Love does not insist on its own way; it is not irritable or resentful; it does not rejoice at wrong, but rejoices in the right. Love bears all things, believes all things, hopes all things, endures all things' (1 Cor. 13:4–7). These words were written by the much maligned Paul, but what he says here about love might be said with equal truth about Jesus Christ or about Mary, and it ought to be possible to say it about any faithful Christian, whether man or woman. In every case, humility and obedience toward God is characteristic, but this must not be confused with fawning submissiveness.

Before we go on to a more directly theological discussion of Mary, it will be helpful to consider in somewhat more detail the phenomenon of human sexuality, and the differences between the sexes. In the first place, of course, there are physical differences, and these differences in human beings correspond to differences which are found very widely among living things. These physical differences constitute a biological phenomenon, and one which has been very valuable in realizing the range of possibilities for each species. But in the case of human beings sexuality has attained dimensions that make it far more than simply a biological phenomenon. It was an eminent biologist, J. Z. Young, who wrote that 'the full sexual relationship includes much more than the particular physical reactions'.[1] Sexuality enters very deeply into the personality and psychological make-up of every human being — more deeply, perhaps, than most of us usually realize. Admittedly, sexual differences are founded on physical differences, but they go far beyond anatomy and physiology, and express themselves in deep mental, personal and spiritual differences.

This has sometimes been denied, and attempts have been made to minimize the differences between the sexes by explaining them in terms of social conditioning rather than as consequences of the biological differences. This was the line taken by some earlier generations of feminists who, though they could scarcely deny the physical differences of the sexes, claimed that there are no inherent differences in mental and personal characteristics. The differences that we have been led to expect, for instance, passivity on the part of women, are said to be due to centuries of cultural conditioning. In short, such characteristics are the result not of nature but of oppression, and if cultural hindrances to the development of women were removed, so it is argued, then the supposed psychological differences between the sexes would gradually disappear. No doubt there is some truth in this point of view. In sexuality, as in other matters, long-established customs set up patterns of behaviour and lead us to form stereotypes to which we expect individuals to conform. We have preconceived ideas of what a man or woman is or ought to be, and how he or she will normally behave, and the tendency is to expect all men and women to fall under these stereotypes. But many of the stereotypes have no validity and are no guide to what a person may do or can do. In the present century, first in wartime and then in peacetime, women have taken over and worked proficiently at jobs once considered suitable only for men, and these women have shown that they have not only the physical skills but the psychological resources, both intellectual and emotional, for performing these jobs well. This notable social advance has been accomplished in the face of considerable hostile prejudice. Nevertheless, when all this has been admitted, intellectual and emotional differences remain, and it is an oversimplification to suppose that they are all due to cultural and historical factors, and that it is all due to prejudice that we have come to think of distinctively masculine and feminine personalities and personality traits. I mentioned an earlier generation of feminists who tried simply to abolish the differences between themselves and men. One can read about them in the writings of Colette. These women dressed like men, talked like men (or as they imagined men talk), followed supposedly masculine sports and recreations and even took female lovers. Such persons are probably no longer to be found and in any case they give an impression of fundamental insecurity rather than of the dignity of women. A naive egalitarianism which simply ignores differences usually ends up by militating against true human worth.

What the more sophisticated feminists of recent years have protested against is not that the sexes are different — this, after all, is something inescapably given — but the idea that the differences are to be interpreted in terms of superiority and inferiority. Many cultures have undoubtedly encouraged the belief that only the male of the species is fully a human being, and that women are somehow incomplete human beings or second-class human beings. Such a belief obviously belongs to what we call the 'law of the jungle', the belief that might is right and that strength in a physical and material sense gives to the strong the right to dominate the weak. Yet in saying that this belief reflects the law of the jungle, it is not meant that it can be found only in primitive societies. It is still in fact widespread over much of the world today. Even in some highly civilized societies, to be born as a female is to begin life with a handicap, occasionally, as is still reported, not to be allowed to live at all.

The prejudice that women are somehow deficient human beings has been given wide and authoritative influence in the west by one of the most celebrated students of the human mind in modern times, Sigmund Freud. According to Freud, the mental development and personality traits of the two sexes are very different indeed, and this difference springs from a natural, physical source. As far as the female is concerned, her whole emotional and personal development is supposed on Freud's theory to be determined by her discovery that she lacks the distinctive sexual organ of the male — by the phenomenon that Freud called 'penis-envy'. To quote his own words: 'Of little girls, we know that they feel themselves heavily handicapped by the absence of a large visible penis and envy the boy's possession of it'.[2] I must leave it to psychologists to decide what evidences there are for and against Freud's theory. All I wish to do is to point out that, beginning from the alleged phenomenon of penis-envy, this influential student of

11

human nature was driven to give a mainly negative account of female psychology. The woman is determined by envy and the frustrating desire to be a man, and therefore also by feelings of inferiority and a latent masochism. I do not mean that Freud was consciously advocating the subjection of women or the denial to them of a fully human status, though his theories about sexuality were bound to encourage such attitudes. We can also acknowledge that he was correct in thinking that there are important psychological differences between the sexes. But what must be opposed in his teaching is the implication that a woman is a deficient human being or inevitably believes herself to be such.

Ann Ulanov, who writes from a Christian and Jungian background, is, in my opinion, much more convincing than Freud. Although she too recognizes the very different styles of masculine and feminine personality, she argues that each needs the other to constitute a complete humanity. The implication is that, taken in isolation, the masculine and the feminine are both deficient. She writes, 'The feminine is half of human wholeness, an essential part of it . . . Masculine and feminine elements exist only in relation to each other, and complement rather than fight each other'.[3] Here the starting-point for considering the relation of the sexes is not envy or a sense of superiority or inferiority on one side or the other, but complementarity and a desire on each side for a wholeness which needs a contribution from each side.

The same writer lays stress on the tendency to embrace things and persons in their wholeness as typical of the feminine style of mentality. The masculine mind is analytical, critical, specialized, discursive; the feminine, by contrast, is aiming at completeness and is intuitive. Of course, such descriptions are generalizations and cannot be used to prejudge particular cases. The contrasts to which they draw attention are probably founded ultimately on the physical differences between the sexes. In this connection, one may mention the work of Erik Erikson. He observed that, given a set of building blocks, girls will use them to construct enclosures in which there is peace and security, while boys tend to construct towers, projections and the like. Erikson saw these activities as reflecting in each case the structure of the children's own bodies. It would be very implausible in such cases to argue that the differences are the result of some kind of social conditioning rather than the consequence of basic physical differences between male and female. Though working in the Freudian tradition, Erikson did not accept Freud's interpretation of the feminine mentality but gave it a positive evaluation. He claimed that it expresses 'a productive inner-bodily space' which is the complement of the outgoing masculine thrust.[4] To the comments of Ulanov and Erikson may be added a point made by the Oxford psychologist, R. S. Lee. He too began from Freudian principles, but came to interesting conclusions about the differences in moral perception between men and women. Boys, he claimed, because of the relation to the father develop a strong superego and come to see morality in terms of rules and ethical principles. Girls have a different relation to the father and come to understand morality more in terms of ideals than of authoritative rules. 'A woman is more practical and positive in her moral decisions than a man, because they are personal rather than abstract, and her judgements are intuitive rather than analytical'.[5] So while it must again be said that these descriptions are generalized and must not be used to prejudge individual cases, they do suggest that some differences in mentality between the sexes are fairly typical, and can be seen as complementary. Neither is superior to the other, and a complete humanity needs the contributions of both.

But now we move on to the important insights of C. J. Jung. In his view, the masculine and feminine types of personality are not found in isolation, the masculine exclusively in men and the feminine exclusively in women. Rather, every human being, whether man or woman, has both masculine and feminine elements in his or her personality. Of course, in most cases the man tends to be more masculine than feminine and the woman to be more feminine than masculine. But every man has his *anima*, that part of his psyche which is the feminine complement of the dominant masculine part, and every woman has her *animus*, the masculine part of her psyche which complements the dominant feminine part.

These brief remarks on human sexuality and the relations of masculine and feminine have now led us to the point where we can see how difficult and complex this whole matter is. We have seen grounds for believing that the difference between masculine and feminine personalities is a real one. We have seen further that it has nothing to do with questions of superiority or inferiority, but rather with the completeness of human life which has to be built out of different elements that will sometimes be in tension with each other. We have also seen that it is possible to characterize the feminine in broad strokes — it is a type of mentality responsive rather than initiating, concerned with the whole, the inward, the ideal, with what can be intuited rather than deduced, while the masculine style is different at each point. But finally we have seen that every well-balanced human being is constituted of both masculine and feminine elements, and that it would be a mere caricature or stereotype to suppose that in every woman one finds or should find exclusively the typically feminine traits, or in every man the corresponding masculine traits.

If we think for a moment of Mary who, it is commonly supposed, has been held up by the Church as a pattern of Christian womanhood, we can indeed see in her the typical feminine characteristics described above. She responds to the initiating activity of God's messenger: 'Be it unto me according to thy word' (Lk. 1:38). She has great inward depth: 'she pondered all these things in her heart' (Lk. 2:19). She has the feminine capacity for patient endurance of pain: 'a sword will pass through your own soul also' (Lk. 2:35). But these quotations by no means exhaust the picture of Mary, even in Luke's gospel, to which I have for the present confined myself. She manifests action as well as passion, and does not hesitate to speak out what is in her mind. So Pope Paul VI, in his Apostolic Exhortation *Marialis Cultus* tried to bring out some of the stronger traits in Mary's personality, no doubt in response to current criticism that she has been made the pattern for womanly submissiveness. In language which I must say strikes me as somewhat quaint, the Pope said: 'The modern woman will appreciate that Mary's choice of the state of virginity was not a rejection of any of the values of the married state, but a courageous choice which she made in order to consecrate herself totally to the love of God. The modern woman will note with pleasant surprise that Mary of Nazareth was far from being a timidly submissive woman; on the contrary, she was a woman who did not hesitate to proclaim that God vindicates the humble and oppressed, and removes the powerful people of this world from their privileged positions'.[6] The later part of this quotation seems to allude quite plainly to the *Magnificat* or Song of Mary (Lk. 1:46–55). Many modern scholars would question whether this ancient canticle does in fact come from Mary, but even if it does not, it has been associated with Mary for so long in Christian tradition that its teaching does now firmly attach to her and influences the way in which she has come to be perceived by Christians. So the Pope was certainly justified in recalling the language of the *Magnificat* and so drawing us away from the stereotype of Mary as weak and altogether submissive. To recall my own language used earlier, Mary was no doormat, no mere nonentity or mindless instrument to be used apart from her own feelings and volitions. However, Popes, like lesser mortals, sometimes find themselves in a no-win situation. The Holy Father's hope that he would (to use his own expression) 'pleasantly surprise' the hypothetical 'modern woman' by unveiling another side of Mary's character was not realized. It seems that when he appealed to the *Magnificat* he proved too much, for one woman critic has claimed that the *Magnificat* has a 'bellicose and triumphalist character'.[7] So perhaps after all one should not strive too officiously to conform Mary to the more aggressive patterns of womanhood now current. Mary cannot be rightly conformed to any stereotype, ancient or modern. In the modern world, Mary can hardly be other than a sign of contradiction, making us aware of a profound conflict between two value-systems.

Let us now return to the question of God and of what place, if any, ideas of sexuality and femininity can have in our understanding of God. Most Christian theologians have believed that, however dimly or obliquely, the infinite is reflected in the finite, so that whatever is good and affirmative in the created order imperfectly mirrors something in God himself, though admittedly that 'something' in God may so transcend what we know in finite existence that there will be incomprehensible difference as well as some measure of affinity. Mystical theologians have always combined analogical language with a considerable measure of agnosticism. Of course, at times when the sexual act was considered inherently sinful and the feminine was in consequence despised or feared, to talk of sexuality or femininity in God would have been branded as unchristian and pagan, perhaps even blasphemous. But if one does set a positive value on sexuality, and if one acknowledges that the masculine and the feminine are essentially the complements of one another in a completely personal human being, and that neither the masculine nor the feminine can claim superiority in their polar relationship, then presumably whatever is good and affirmative in sexuality and in femininity is present in an eminent way in God. This does not mean that God has a sex in the ordinary sense of the word. He is beyond distinction of male and female. Though we habitually use masculine words to refer to God, Christian faith acknowledges that God transcends sex, but he does so not by sheerly excluding sexuality but by including in the divine nature in an eminent way whatever is of value in sexuality. Some of these questions have been explored with truly remarkable insight by Karl Barth in his treatment of the creation stories in Genesis, and I shall be turning to them shortly.

But since I have mentioned the habitual use of masculine pronouns to refer to God, it may be appropriate at this point to say more about this and to ask whether this practice is justifiable. I think we have first of all to acknowledge — and I think most theologians and philosophers of religion would agree — that all our language about God is inadequate. God cannot be captured and described in the categories of finite thought, so we speak of him either in negatives or indirectly by means of analogies, metaphors, symbols of various kinds. On the particular question of what pronouns are appropriate when speaking of God, it is important to distinguish clearly between grammatical gender and actual differences of sex. Although masculine nouns and pronouns usually refer to males, and feminine words to females, this is not always the case. In English, grammatical gender has been reduced to minimal importance, and the vast majority of words are neuter. In most other languages, even the names of things have gender, though most of the things so named have no sexual characteristics. Presumably this is the legacy of a more mythological age when the powers of nature, for instance, were personified and even deified. Even so, there is no

17

consistency in such matters. In many languages, the word for 'sun' is masculine and the word for 'moon' is feminine, but there are many other languages in which this situation is reversed. Such accidents of language have no more than a superficial influence (if even that) on the feeling that people have for the referends. A Frenchman does not think of the sun as male because *le soleil* is a masculine expression, nor does a German think of it as female because *die Sonne* is a feminine word. To give a somewhat different example, the Hebrews customarily used a plural noun, *elohim*, for God, but this did not affect their strict monotheism, and even in their grammar they did not think it inconsistent to use for God singular pronouns and singular verb forms.

I mention these matters because we must be clear that there is a big difference between grammatical conventions and matters of biological fact. In particular, I do not think anything is to be gained by the habit in some quarters of referring to God (or goddess?) as 'she'. When this is done, the somewhat startling departure from habitual linguistic usage throws an emphasis on the feminine gender of the pronoun and inevitably suggests a literal femininity in God. If one is seeking to correct popular misconceptions of God as a male, this purpose will not be served by linguistic innovations but only by sound teaching. I think we have a good example of such teaching in Julian of Norwich who avoided linguistic gimmicks but nevertheless got across the idea that the mystery of God can find expression in feminine as well as masculine imagery. Here are two examples: 'And so I saw that God rejoices that he is our Father, and God rejoices that he is our mother, and God rejoices that he is our true spouse'; and again, even more paradoxically, she says,

So Jesus Christ, who opposes good to evil, is our true Mother. We have our being from him from whom true motherhood begins, with all the sweet protection of love which endlessly follows.[8]

I have spoken here of 'sound teaching' and suggested that if we had more of that, it would promote a better understanding of God than attempts to change the customary linguistic forms. To explore further what the 'sound teaching' is, we turn to the two creation stories of Genesis, and in them we find a wealth of helpful material.

Let us begin with the older and more pronounced by mythological of these stories, the one which now appears in the second chapter of Genesis. I have already granted that there are some elements in this story which might be interpreted as suggesting the subordination of the woman — she is created subsequently to Adam, she is intended to be his helper, and, in the continuation, she is the first to fall into sin. But the main point of the story is surely quite different. The main point is that Adam remains an incomplete being until the creation of Eve. This is the story-teller's way of making the point that, in language that has been used from Feuerbach to Buber, there is no 'I' without a 'thou', or in slightly different language, there can be no personal self that is not related to another self. And, as Karl Barth has pointed out, it is sexuality (according to the Genesis story) which is the original form of the interpersonal relation. Sexuality is 'the basic form of all association and fellowship, which is the essence of humanity'.[9] Indeed, in Barth's view, it is sociality and therefore fundamentally sexuality which constitutes the image of God in humanity.

Why is sexuality so interpreted? I should say myself that it is because the sexual relation is the most intimate act of mutual self-giving and communion possible for two human beings. Indeed, can we still speak of 'two'? Or have they become in a sense a new whole — 'one flesh' in the biblical language? This point is reinforced when we consider even the physical factors in themselves. Every individual human being is, in large measure, a self-contained unit. He or she seems to have everything necessary for life — a complete respiratory system, cardiovascular system, nervous system, alimentary system and so on — but only one half of a reproductive system which needs completion by another.

It will be noted too that the first words which Adam speaks are addressed to the woman. Language, which sets the distance between human being and merely animal being, is basic to human association and fellowship, and it is evoked from Adam by Eve in his meeting with her.

But it is in the later and more sophisticated account of the creation, now in the first chapter of Genesis, that we see more clearly how the human sexual relation has significance for the understanding of God. As the climax of his great creative work, God says,

> Let us make man in our image, after our likeness . . . So God created man in his own image, in the image of God created he him; male and female created he them (Gn. 1:26–7).

In this story, man and woman are created simultaneously, and thus their equality and co-essentiality to humanity are recognized. But what is more important is that both the man and the woman are required for the possibility of an image of God on the level of the finite. The image is jointly constituted by man and woman in their 'one flesh'. The image is reflected in their community, which requires in turn their sexuality, so that we conclude that the image of God needs both masculinity and femininity.

Commentators have sometimes drawn attention to the fact that, contrary to the grammatical convention which I mentioned above, the verb used by God, 'Let us make . . .', is plural, not singular. The fact that the Hebrew word for

God is grammatically plural in form, though singular in meaning, is being exploited at this point. If association and fellowship are essential to personal being, and if God is the supreme or eminent person, then there must be distinctions or diversity within God, God is not a bare individual being but is self-related. Or to put it in another way, there must be sociality in God. Many centuries after the Hebrew scriptures were written, Christian theologians worked out the doctrine of the Trinity, the teaching that God is perfectly one yet at the same time self-related, so that within the unity are the three distinct modes of being that we call Father, Son and Holy Spirit. Though such ideas were far from the minds of the writers of Genesis, it is not wrong to see in these writings some foreshadowings of the doctrine of God as it came to be rethought in the light of the revelation in Jesus Christ. Is there any better analogy we can find for representing to ourselves (so far as we can understand it) the mystery of the three-in-one and one-in-three of the Triune God than the earthly mystery of Christian marriage, in which two become one flesh — and, in a sense, this is also a trinity, for in sacramental marriage God is the ever-present third party in the love that unites husband and wife, and is indeed the life of both. In the sexual relation, the partners are distinct, and yet they are one, and that is surely our best clue to understanding what theologians have meant by the *perichoresis* or *circumincessio* of the divine persons of the Trinity, that is to say, their mutual interpenetration and reciprocity.

Such reciprocity clearly implies that there are in God, as the consummation and perfect integration of the individual and social poles of personal being, elements analogous to both feminine and masculine. Sometimes attempts have been made to associate the feminine element with a particular person of the Trinity, namely, the Holy Spirit.[10] The Spirit's brooding on the creation suggests the

21

contemplative inner space of the feminine, while the Spirit's travail amid the sighs of creation suggests the feminine work of bringing to birth through patient endurance. But just as in human marriage each partner evinces both masculine and feminine characteristics, so the analogues of those characteristics belong to all three persons of the Trinity. As we have seen, Julian of Norwich did not hesitate to speak of motherhood in relation to the Father and the Son.

There is a further point worth mentioning in this discussion. The union of husband and wife is not a closed union — it opens out into the wider community of the family. In the sexual union, man and woman under God become procreators, they are charged with the solemn and joyful task of creating community. Although modern techniques have made it possible to separate the activities of sexual intercourse and reproduction, we must never lose sight of the essential connection between them. In saying this, I am not for a moment denying that there may be benefits in the practice of *in vitro* fertilization if it enables a childless couple to attain to parenthood, nor am I denying that acts of intercourse not explicitly aimed at reproduction have a place in cementing the relation of the marriage partners. But such practices receive their justification within the context of the normal and natural relation of sexuality and reproduction. Human procreation is a reflection of God's own creativity. God was not content, so to speak, to stay within himself or to enjoy the untroubled bliss of his unique individual-cum-social being. His creation is the generous overflow of his love. But when God created out of love finite persons, he thereby made himself vulnerable to his creation, for there can be no love without vulnerability. In spite of the traditional doctrine of the impassibility of God, many theologians today believe that they must speak of some reciprocity in the relation between God and the world, and even that they must speak of God's suffering in and with his creatures. Creation itself already implies a cross, and the same kind of shadow is reflected in the human family. So again in some respects it is being recognized that the life of God has to be envisaged in feminine as well as masculine terms. Indeed, a deeper recognition of the feminine in God will surely be, both intellectually and spiritually, an enrichment of the human relation to God.

But how is this desired end to be achieved? For those who are seeking a solution within the resources of the Christian tradition, there can be no question of a return to polytheistic religion or any kind of paganism, in which one or more goddesses are set alongside him whom the Bible recognizes as the one true God. Nor would it be acceptable to imagine or represent God in androgynous or hermaphrodite form, as Siva is sometimes represented in Indian art,[11] for although this makes a point that has some validity, it takes the idea of sexuality in God far too literally, reducing God to the level of a finite being and infringing the mystery of God and the gulf between the infinite and the finite. Some of the more extreme feminist sects have chosen to revive the figure of the goddess, but those who want to remain within the Christian tradition must look for another way.

It is here, I think, we must look again at the Christian tradition about Mary, as it has been expressed both in spirituality and theology. As was said much earlier in this chapter, corrections in Christian theology are usually best made not by violent innovations but by recovering corrective tendencies within the tradition itself. I believe that study of the Marian tradition can help Christians to reach a fuller and more balanced understanding of the feminine in their religion, from the theological question about the significance of sexuality for our understanding of God to practical questions about the roles of women in the modern Church. Obviously some parts of that tradition need to be rethought

23

and where necessary corrected, though not necessarily along the lines of *Marialis Cultus*.

Perhaps the first step toward a new appreciation of Mary is just to affirm quite emphatically and unambiguously that she is an entirely human person. Whatever honours may have been paid to Mary in Christian history, however exaggerated some of the acts of veneration may have been, she is not a goddess, she has no more than a human nature (unlike her Son, who is said to have also a divine nature), she is not a person of the Trinity (which would have to be expanded to a Quaternity). She is no more, no less, than a woman — a human being of the female sex. The theological situation of mariology today is parallel to the situation of christology — we have to get back to the human reality of Mary, just as in christology theologians have been getting back to the true humanity of Jesus Christ. There is nothing reductionist in this return to humanity. Is not humanity that item in the created order where there is manifested the image of God? Is not the 'divinity' of Jesus to be seen only in his humanity?

But why do we say 'only'? Whether we are speaking of Christ or Mary, the word 'only' is quite mistakenly taken in a reductionist way, but it can be understood and should be understood as affirmation in the fullest sense. I said above, Mary is 'no more, no less, than a woman'. 'No more', because she is not a goddess, hence not a mythological figment, but a real person; 'no less', because there is no more honourable term we could find for her, and with her we begin to understand the depth, fullness and mystery of womanhood, and therefore of humanity, of which woman-hood is an essential and co-equal expression with manhood.

As we shall see, the Church has from early times restrained its enthusiasts from such excesses of Marian devotion as would tend to place her 'beyond' womanhood, for that would be in fact a depreciation of Mary, who would then be no longer a glorious creation of God but a product of the pagan urge to produce gods and goddesses in the image of our own desires. Even the most exalted titles which the Church has used of Mary are to be understood in terms of her fully human existence as a woman. Perhaps the most exalted title of all is 'Mother of God'. In the form *Theotokos* this title is also very ancient, having been in use at least from the third century. The greatest Protestant theologian of modern times, Karl Barth, has forthrightly declared: 'The description of Mary as "Mother of God" was and is sensible, permissible and necessary as an auxiliary christological proposition'.[12] These words are worth pondering, especially as they come from a theologian who has been jealous in guarding the unique place of Jesus Christ in Christian faith and has been suspicious of mariology as a possible threat to the principle *sola gratia*. Certainly, there is no question of Mary as 'Mother of God' being identified with some primeval metaphysical or mythological source of being, from which are sprung even God or the gods — like the Great Goddess of pre-Hellenic Aegean civilization, or figures such as Gaia (the earth goddess) or Tethys (the spouse of Oceanus) who appear in Hesiod's *Theogony*, that mythological account of the origins of the gods and of the cosmos. Mary can be rightly called 'Mother of God' only in the strictly Christian sense that she is the mother of Jesus Christ, whom the Church confesses as Son of God and an equal person of the divine Trinity. Yet even when we understand the expression 'Mother of God' in the specifically Christian sense (founded in christology), it remains a highly exalted title, readily susceptible to misunderstanding, and one can understand the uneasiness it causes among some Protestants who are neither so bold nor as theologically informed as Karl Barth.

The title is highly exalted because it puts in the strongest imaginable language the indispensable part which

Mary played, as a human being and a woman, in the economy of salvation. If there was to be an incarnation, then there had to be a woman as the necessary agent. And obviously it could not be just any woman, as if all that mattered was the conceiving and bearing of a child. It had to be a woman singularly 'graced' or 'favoured' of God (Lk. 1:28 and 30). She had to conceive him not only in her womb but in her heart, she had not only to bring the child forth but to rear him, to awaken him as any mother must to the meaning of love, to impart to him a constant orientation to God, and these things were possible only if she lived herself in the closest relation to God (that is, in grace) and was perfectly responsive to him. In other words, she had to be truly and utterly woman.

At the risk of labouring the point, I say again, Mary was not a goddess. She is not the Word incarnate, but the Bearer of the Word. Perhaps this fits her more than any other status could to be an exemplar and liberator for women, to manifest the greatness and glory of womanhood. Historically, the cult of goddesses has not been conducive to a higher status for women. But Mary is through and through human, and therefore she can be an example for Christians, men as well as women. Since Vatican II, the title 'Mother of the Church' has taken its place alongside the older title 'Mother of God', and this does show a certain shift in the understanding of Mary. As 'Mother of the Church' she stands firmly on the human side as a member (albeit the pre-eminent member) of the redeemed community. Christ himself, by contrast, is the Redeemer. Admittedly, we can talk about the 'imitation' of Christ and hold up his example, but primarily he is Lord and Saviour, and so receives the full tribute of worship, rather than being venerated as an exemplar. However, Mary's own unique and indispensable role as the God-Bearer and the way in which her life was enveloped and formed by God and by the Son of God, imparted to her a quite special degree of sanctity. In her, the Church claims to have seen what the divine grace can achieve in a human life that has been surrendered to God. We can say that in effecting his work of salvation, God has put at the very heart of it his 'handmaid' (Lk. 1:38) and has thus made the feminine an essential medium in the communication of himself to his creation.

Of course, all this calls for further exploration. But we can say that if we allow the feminine to enter into our thinking about God, this will be an enrichment of our relation to him. And we can also believe that, as has happened in the past, the enlarged understanding of God will be greatly advanced by the place that we give in theology and spirituality to the handmaid of the Lord, the Blessed Virgin Mary.

Notes

1. J. Z. Young, *An Introduction to the Study of Man* (Oxford University Press, 1971), p. 186.
2. Sigmund Freud, *Introductory Lectures on Psychoanalysis* (Allen & Unwin, 1933), p. 267.
3. Ann Ulanov, *The Feminine* (Northwestern University Press, 1971), pp. 156, 164.
4. Erik Erikson, 'Inner and Outer Space: Reflections on Womanhood, in *The Woman in America*, ed R. J. Lifton (Houghton Mifflin Co., 1965), quoted in Ulanov p. 151.
5. R. S. Lee, 'Human Nature and the Fall', in *Man, Fallen and Free*, ed. E. Kemp (Hodder & Stoughton, 1969), p. 54.
6. *Marialis Cultus* (Catholic Truth Society, 1974), pp. 62–3.
7. Marina Warner, *Alone of All Her Sex* (Weidenfeld and Nicholson, 1976), p. 13.
8. Julian of Norwich, *Showings* (Paulist Press, 1978), pp. 279, 295.
9. Karl Barth, *Church Dogmatics* III/1 (T. & T. Clark, 1958), p. 288.
10. See my book, *Thinking about God* (SCM Press, 1975), especially Chapter 11.
11. As, for instance, in the famous sculptures on Elephant Island, near Bombay.
12. Karl Barth, Church Dogmatics I/2 (T. & T. Clark, 1956), p. 138.

2　Mary in the New Testament

What do we really know about Mary? Do we know enough
for her to have any place in Christian theology or devotion?
Since the end of the nineteenth century, we have been
hearing from New Testament critics that our information
even about Jesus Christ is quite scanty. If this is the case with
the central figure in the New Testament, what are we to say
about a marginal figure, such as Mary? She seems to get
mentioned only incidentally, and from the fragments
available, it seems to be impossible to put together a
consistent picture. Of course, neither in the case of Jesus nor
in that of Mary is theology concerned only with facts of
history, but with these facts as they have been subjected to
reflection and incorporated into a body of beliefs concerning
God's self-communication with his creatures in and through
these facts. But it has always been felt important to maintain
the link with historical factuality. The story of the Christ-
event, which includes not only the story of Jesus but the
story of those associated with him in the event, Mary as well
as others, is not, so Christians believe, just a product of the
pious imagination but has its origin in real happenings,
though it would not be denied that in course of time the
happenings have been embellished with legendary material,
intended to bring out the deeper significance of the events
concerned. Inevitably one is bound to posit at the centre of
these events a human being who must have been born, have
grown up and so on; but by the time anyone came to narrate

the story of these matters, it was already set in a context of angels, celestial phenomena and suchlike marvels. In the case of Mary, has not the historical element entirely disappeared, so that we are left only with a tapestry of legends which even the early generations of Christians were soon able to distinguish as 'apocrypha' from those reports which they recognized as corresponding to the apostolic kerygma and came to regard as 'canonical'?

I think we have to answer this question by saying, 'Not quite'. Some few traces of the 'historical' Mary have come through — some sharp edges, if you like, which have not been smoothed to fit into the developing picture and which even today cause some embarrassment to the advocates of mariology. I mean those scenes in the gospel where there seems to be quite a sharp tension between Mary and her Son, and which we shall discuss later. In principle, the problem with regard to Mary is not different from that which arises with regard to Jesus. There is a somewhat meagre amount of historical information — much more meagre in the case of Mary than in that of Jesus. Out of this has developed a body of theological teaching. The 'facts', as suggested above, get incorporated into imaginative stories in which they are understood as vehicles of theological truth, or, as I have expressed it elsewhere, the 'facts' are presented as 'mysteries',[1] events that belong in one sense to history, but in another are 'revelations', events that open up the truth of God. One of the tasks of the theologian is to inquire into this process. What grounds are there for the theological developments that have taken place in the history of the Church? How can we be sure that such developments are genuine *developments* in the sense that they are drawing out resources of truth and meaning that were already latent in the given material, and are not simply moving into new inventions or even corruptions? From time to time in Christian history, theologians have felt it necessary to go back to the sources of the Christian revelation to check whether there is an adequate basis there for the later developments. This is something we have to do in the case of mariology, for, as already noted, the biblical material is quite scanty in comparison with the sometimes elaborate doctrines that have arisen, especially within the last century and a half. Part of the trouble is that in spite of the sceptical ideas that we have inherited from the Enlightenment, we moderns tend to read the New Testament as seen through two thousand years of Christian theology. And I should add, not just Christian theology but Christian spirituality and Christian art. Is not this especially the case with Mary? We have all admired and been touched by these wonderful pictures by generations of Europe's finest artists from the Middle Ages onward — pictures of the annunciation, of the assumption, of the wedding at Cana, of the finding of Jesus in the Temple, and so on and so on. These pictures convey so much spiritual truth that we make a willing 'suspension of disbelief' if the question, 'What really happened?' arises in our minds. Perhaps we are right to turn away from any crude literalism. But we cannot have it both ways. Are these simply poetic fantasies in which the human mind soars into realms of spiritual aspiration? Or are they rooted in the Christ-event, already concealed in that revelatory event from which Christianity took its rise and to which the New Testament writers witness?

The New Testament material on Mary is so small in bulk that even in this brief chapter, we shall be able to review virtually all of it. When we have done that, it should be clearer to us what kind of foundation is available on which to construct a theology of Mary, and perhaps also whether it is worthwhile to attempt the task. For even if mariological doctrines can be theologically justified, might they not be just a confusion, a luxuriant development that would be better pruned back lest it obscure the essential elements in Christian faith? So would argue some of the Protestant critics of mariology, and we may concede that some of the excesses in the cult of Mary have given weight to their criticisms. But that does not rule out the possibility that there are forms of Marian theology and devotion which can constitute an enrichment of Christianity. But to learn whether this is the case, we begin by going back to the New Testament evidence concerning Mary.

If we consider this evidence in chronological order, we must begin with the letters of Paul, the oldest documents in the New Testament. This will not delay us long, for in the whole corpus of the Pauline letters, there is only one mention of Mary — in fact, she is not even named. Paul, of course, included very little historical information of any kind in his letters. His task was to expound faith and theology, and only very occasionally does he insert a mention of an incident in the life of Jesus.[2] What he says concerning Mary is hardly an historical remark, for although it mentions an event that has happened in history, it offers no description of the event and it is mentioned primarily for its theological significance. The passage, to be dated probably to the early fifties, reads as follows:

> But when the time had fully come, God sent forth his son, born of a woman, born under the law, to redeem those who were under the law, so that we might receive adoption as sons (Gal. 4:4–5).

Obviously, the 'woman' in this passage is Mary, the mother of Jesus, but perhaps Paul did not know her name. Indeed, there is no reason to suppose he had any information about the birth at all. As I said, this is hardly a historical statement at all, but a theological one. Jesus was 'born of a woman', that is to say, he was truly and genuinely a human being, and he was 'born under the law', which may simply be

31

reinforcing the point that he truly shared our human condition, for the human race is 'under the law' and, according to Paul's teaching in this letter, alienated from its true destiny. So the teaching here seems to be that being born of a woman into the human race, Christ stands in solidarity with all human beings. Only so would it be possible for him to 'redeem' those who are under the law. But Paul did not need any historical information to write these words. They are theologically self-evident, or, to go even further, one could say they are just plain common sense. It seems clear too that Paul had never heard of a virgin birth. He says of Jesus simply that he was 'born of a woman'. It will be at least thirty years after Paul's letter before the gospels of Matthew and Luke report a virgin birth. One must ask whether Paul's argument here is compatible with a virgin birth (or virginal conception). For if we are correct in thinking that Paul is wanting to stress the solidarity of Jesus with the human race, would not this be placed in doubt by a virginal conception?

There is another important theological point in the passage quoted from Paul. It lies in the words 'when the time had fully come', or, to translate more literally, 'when the fullness of the time was come'. What is meant by the 'fullness of the time?' Clearly, a definite understanding of history lies behind this expression. All times are not alike, events do not follow one another haphazardly. Paul believed that there is a providential ordering in history, and in particular that God himself is working out some salvific plan. This belief was not peculiar to Paul, but one that he shared with many people in the ancient world, not only fellow Christians but Jews and some of the pagan philosophers as well. The 'fullness of the time' would seem to designate a climax in the history of Israel. If from the calling of Abraham onward God had been preparing and educating his people to be the agent of his good purpose, then in Paul's belief that process had come to its decisive moment with the conception and birth of Jesus Christ. The belief (which is perhaps in some form inevitable for any Christian who accepts that Jesus Christ is the signal revelation of God in history) is that he appeared at the time when he did not just by chance or by some unaccountable quirk of evolution but as the fulfilment of a creative striving or nisus that had been going on through history and prehistory, a nisus having its origin in God and now at last finding its expression in the world. In more theological language, we could speak, as does Barth, for example, of election and predestination, by which is meant that from the beginning God had predestined Jesus Christ to his vocation as inaugurator of the kingdom of God and of the new humanity. But if Jesus Christ was so elected, then so were those who had been links in the historical chain leading to Jesus Christ — the human race itself had been elected, within the human race the people of Israel had been elected, and within Israel Mary was elected as the last link in the chain before the appearance of the Christ. So even if Paul does not give us any historical information about Mary, his brief reference to her sets in motion an important train of thought concerning her place in the divine purpose and in the drama of salvation.

After Paul, our oldest source of information is the gospel of Mark, written perhaps twelve or fifteen years after the letter to the Galatians. Mark knows that Jesus' mother was called Mary, though he uses her name only once. But although he says very little about her, what he says fits in so badly with what came to be the conventional view of Mary that it does have the ring of historical truth about it. It fits in badly because Mark shows us not the devoted mother encouraging and supporting her son in his mission, but seems rather to suggest that there was considerable tension between the two of them. Mark, of course, has no birth narrative and passes over the early years of Jesus in complete silence. The curtain rises as he already begins his ministry, and it is early in the ministry that we meet the figure of Mary.

Let me just recall the significant incidents. The first is perhaps the most embarrassing of all — so embarrassing that Matthew and Luke, who usually repeat Mark's narrative, have left out this particular incident. Jesus, we are told, had gone home and a crowd had gathered around, presumably in expectation of healing miracles or to hear the teaching. Emotions were running high, there may have been some disorder, 'they could not even eat'. At this point, we are told, 'when his family heard of it, they went out to seize him, for people were saying. "He is beside himself"' (Mk. 3:19b–21). Mary is not actually named here, though it is probable that she would be included in 'his family'. What the incident seems to show is a pretty complete misunderstanding between Jesus and the members of his family. To put it crudely, they thought he was mad. Later in the same chapter comes another incident, in which the mother and brothers of Jesus seem once again to misunderstand what he is about, while he for his part brushes them off.

> And his mother and his brothers came; and standing outside, they sent to him and called him. And a crowd was sitting about him; and they said to him, 'Your mother and your brothers are outside asking for you'. And he replied, 'Who are my mother and my brothers?' And looking around on those who sat about him, he said, 'Here are my mother and my brothers! Whoever does the will of God is my brother, and sister and mother' (Mk. 3:31–5).

On still another occasion, he visits his home territory. But now he is taunted by the townspeople, who know his family. 'Is not this the carpenter, the son of Mary and brother of

James and Joses and Judas and Simon, and are not his sisters here with us?' (Mk. 6:3). The townspeople were offended because Jesus, whose antecedents they knew so well, was setting himself up as a teacher. Jesus himself felt constrained to say, 'A prophet is not without honour, except in his own country, and among his own kin, and in his own house' (Mk. 6:4). The implication of these words seems quite clear. Jesus' claims as a teacher were rejected by the people who knew him best, including his own family. Matthew and Luke do have parallels telling of this rejection of Jesus by the people of his home town, and Luke describes something approaching a riot in which an attempt is made to kill Jesus. But neither of these evangelists repeat Mark's report that Jesus had complained that even his own kin and his own household rejected him.

Why do we find the idea that Jesus was not accepted, or not immediately accepted, by his family so embarrassing? After all, he did seem to be correct in his general claim that a prophet has no honour in his own country. It is a well-known fact that a person whom we know familiarly is not likely to be a person for whom we develop any feeling of awe. But in the case of Jesus, we do find these incidents embarrassing because we are reading them in the light of what we have learned from other sources. We all know the much-loved story of the annunciation in Luke's gospel; of how the archangel Gabriel appeared to Mary and announced that she would conceive a child, and that this child would be great and would be called the Son of the most High, and would inherit the throne of David and rule over Israel. If Mary knew all this from the very beginning, why were she and her family unable to understand what Jesus was about when he embarked on his ministry? What we forget is that although we know the story of the annunciation, Mark did not know it, or certainly gives no indication of having known it. Furthermore, we have to remember that Mark was writing about twenty years before Luke so that the tradition preserved by Mark is likely to be an older one than what we find in Luke. Indeed, if one had to choose between these two authors, I think one would have to say that Mark's account of the rather awkward relationship between Jesus and his mother and the rest of the family has a considerably better claim to be historically trustworthy than has Luke's story. The latter looks, one must say, like the kind of embellishment which grows around an incident when it is recalled at a much later date.

So what are we to say in the light of this Marcan material, throwing as it appears to do a shadow over the relations between Jesus and his mother? Does this ancient testimony rule out mariology right at the beginning of our inquiry? I do not think we need come quite so quickly to such a drastic conclusion, but we have to look for some explanation if we are to proceed any further. I think there are two possible ways of reading these Marcan incidents, and that both ways leave open the path to consequent developments in mariology.

The first possibility is as follows (and let us remember that both possibilities are only hypotheses). Let us suppose that Mary did know of Jesus' vocation and was in sympathy with it — that she had even by bringing him up in the best aspirations of Judaism encouraged that vocation. Inevitably there would be some conflict in her mind. Her motherly instinct would want to protect Jesus, for the way that he was choosing was one of danger; yet her faith in God would make her want to encourage him in his career. So for both Mary and Jesus, it must have been very difficult to reach a right relation to each other. Each of them had to eliminate everything savouring of a possessive love, each had even to sacrifice natural affection for the sake of a higher love, a love consisting not in any kind of possessiveness but in 'letting the other be',[3] in letting and helping the other to fulfil the unique role for which God had elected that person. As Mary and Jesus worked out this very special relation between them, a love-relation transcending all ordinary filial relations, there were bound to be some moments of tension, as still reflected in the gospel record.

The second possibility is slightly different from the one just described. Let us now suppose that Jesus' vocation was not understood by Mary and the family, and that to begin with, they actually opposed it, as for instance when they tried forcibly to restrain him, supposing that he had become unbalanced. One could hardly say they were acting wrongly, indeed, they were acting out of a mistaken kind of love. But let us suppose that in course of time they came to understand Jesus and his vocation better. After all, did not Jesus himself grow in the understanding of who he was and what was required of him? There is a possible scrap of evidence which would favour this line of explanation. One of Jesus' brothers was called James, and the evidence in Mark shows that James was among those family members who opposed Jesus in the early days of his ministry. But at some point — how soon or how late, we do not know — James had a change of heart, and is named by Paul (Gal. 2:9) and by the author of Acts (15:13) as leader or bishop of the church in Jerusalem. Mary too (Acts 1:14) appears as a member of the believing community in contrast to the ambiguous attitude ascribed to her by Mark. If the sequence of events was indeed something like this, it has often been repeated in Christian history, where parents who have helped to implant a love of the Christian faith in a son or daughter are at first opposed to the wish of the child to become a missionary or join a religious order, knowing that they may never see that child again. But in time they are able to accept the idea and even begin to have a certain joy in sharing in the sacrifice. In the case of Mary too, must there not have been a process of learning and adjustment as Jesus' vocation and its possible

37

consequences began to unfold itself? According to the New Testament, Jesus Christ was himself tempted throughout his career, from the temptations in the wilderness at the beginning to the very last hours in Gethsemane. Must there not have been temptations too in the life of Mary, if indeed we can call them 'temptations' — the natural desire of a loving mother to protect her son from whatever might threaten him? What a hard demand was made on her — one is reminded of the words which Luke attributes to the aged Simeon: 'A sword will pierce through your own soul also' (Lk. 2:35). But by the end of the story, Mary's questions have been faced and overcome, and we see her joining in the prayers of the first community of Christians as they await the coming of the Holy Spirit (Acts 1:14).

As we have seen, Mark's gospel presents us with a somewhat ambiguous picture of Mary and her relation to Jesus, though we have also seen this ambiguity can be interpreted in a number of ways. The gospels of Matthew and Luke echo the Marcan material, but tone it down somewhat — they omit that strange incident when the family tried to remove Jesus from the crowd because people were saying he was beside himself, and although they agree that the people of his home town Nazareth gave him an unfriendly reception, they do not follow Mark in including Jesus' family among the opponents. But Matthew and Luke both add new material to what we find in Mark, and this new material opens up new areas for theological reflection on Mary. First, we note that both Matthew and Luke probe back beyond the beginning of Jesus' ministry to give an account of his birth and parentage. The stories which the two evangelists tell are different and obviously come from different sources. But there are two points in common. *Historically,* both gospels place the birth of Jesus in the reign of Herod the Great. He died in 4 BC by our calendar, so that this evidence points to an approximate date for the birth of

Jesus. It was not later than 4 BC and may well have been two or three years earlier, so that in any case it took place several years before the conventional date on which our calendars are based. But apart from the historical point, there is an item of *theological* teaching on which the two evangelists are in agreement. This is their teaching that Jesus was virginally conceived by his mother. What they say about this shows again that they are drawing on different sources. In Matthew's story, an angel appears to Joseph, to whom Mary has been betrothed, and tells him that 'that which is conceived in her is of the Holy Spirit' (Mt. 1:20), so that her pregnancy is not due to any moral lapse but to God's action. In Luke's more detailed story, an angel appears directly to Mary and tells her that she will conceive through the Holy Spirit (Lk. 1:31 and 35). Luke among the evangelists has a special interest in and respect for Mary, and in his account he includes the memorable and often quoted words in which she gives her consent to the high but hazardous vocation to which the angel in the name of God has called her: 'Behold, I am the handmaid of the Lord; let it be to me according to your word' (Lk. 1:38).

The doctrine of the virgin birth (or, more accurately, virginal conception) of Jesus is more significant for christology than for mariology, but I shall not discuss the christological aspects here since I have treated them in my book *Jesus Christ in Modern Thought*.[4] But whether we are considering the implications of the doctrine for christology or mariology, it is important to remember to give priority to its theological interpretation. A great many controversies and questionings over virgin birth could have been avoided if attention had been concentrated on theological questions rather than being diverted to questions of biology. Theologically, we are being told that the birth of Jesus is a redemptive act of God, the creation of a new humanity or the re-creation of a true humanity. The point is brought out

39

very clearly in John's gospel, though there it is not confined to Jesus himself but expanded to include those who are joined with him in the new humanity. For John declares that

> to all who received him, who believed in his name, he gave power to become children of God; who were born, not of blood nor of the will of the flesh nor of the will of man, but of God (Jn. 1:12–13).

This is the inner meaning of 'virgin birth'. I have said that the idea has been expanded to include the members of the new Christian community. But we are concerned for the moment especially with what it says about Mary. She has a central role in the matter — indeed, in Matthew and Luke, she is represented as the sole human agent in the generation of Jesus. So already in the first century, already in two of the canonical gospels, Mary is being accorded a unique and highly exalted place in salvation-history, though always in subordination to her Son, for whose sake she was elected by God. Especially when we consider Luke's narrative, including both the address of the angel and the affirmative response of Mary, it is perhaps not going too far to say that here we already have some pointers to the very much later idea of Mary as *Corredemptrix*, for she is already recognized as the pre-eminent human agent in those events which led to the birth of Jesus and the coming into being of that new humanity of which he is both the first member and the source. Is the honour accorded to Mary in these virgin birth stories an exaggerated one? We shall consider this question in a later chapter, but here I simply want to repeat what I have already urged in other connections, that the honour given to Mary is at the same time an honouring of womanhood. Even those who would be reluctant to accept any literal or biological interpretation of virgin birth will hardly deny that the stories give to Mary a specially exalted place in salvation-history, emphasizing and reiterating Paul's point that in the fullness of the time 'God sent his Son, born of a woman'. Now that woman is exhibited in a special light as the Woman, the new Eve.

Both Matthew and Luke include in their gospels not just birth stories but brief incidents from Jesus' childhood. Matthew tells the stories of the visit to Jesus of the wise men, the rage of Herod and the flight of the Holy Family into Egypt. Mary is mentioned in these incidents, but there does not seem to be anything of importance to note here. As we have seen, it is Luke who of all the evangelists has most interest in Mary and presents the fullest and most sympathetic portrait of her. We have already noted Mary's encounter with the old man Simeon when she presented the child Jesus in the Temple, and some of the words which Simeon uttered then. 'A sword will pierce through your soul also', seem to indicate that Luke is already drawing attention to the fact that Mary will share in the sufferings of her Son. Later in the same chapter Luke tells the story of how the twelve-year-old Jesus was lost by his parents on a visit to Jerusalem, and was eventually found in the Temple, eagerly absorbing the teaching that he heard there. It seems clear that Mary did not understand what was going on: 'Son, why have you treated us so? Behold, your father and I have been looking for you anxiously' (Lk. 2:48). If one wants to accept as historical the earlier story when the angel explains to Mary her vocation and who her unborn child will turn out to be, then presumably she would have remembered what he had said, and so she should not have been surprised when Jesus went off to the temple to learn something about the questions to which he was to devote his life. But Mary is surprised and even somewhat upset at the course of action which the boy had taken. We can only conclude that the tradition we found in Mark, namely, that the family of Jesus, including his mother, were slow to accept and appreciate his special vocation was a strong one and well-known. Thus Luke feels bound to make some mention of the misunderstanding and even tension between Mary and Jesus, in spite of his general sympathy toward Mary and the earlier passages in the gospel in which Mary has been admitted to a knowledge of God's purpose both for Jesus and for herself. We have here two conflicting traditions, and they have not been fully reconciled and perhaps could not be. On the one hand, there is the stubborn tradition, predominant in Mark, residual in Luke, that Mary and the family did not at first understand what was going on in Jesus' mind. On the other hand, when Luke was writing his account eighty or ninety years after the childhood of Jesus, he saw everything in retrospect, he knew the path that led through mission and teaching to suffering and death and finally to resurrection and ascension. He believed that all this had come about by the providential decree of God. So must not Mary and Jesus have been given an understanding of God's plan? Must they not have been carrying it out consciously? There is a parallel to this in the way in which Mark and the other synoptic evangelists represent Jesus' words to the disciples, predicting his own death and resurrection. Several times, according to Mark, he warns them in explicit detail of what will happen. But when the time comes, they are taken utterly by surprise. The explanation offered by most New Testament scholars is that the predictions ascribed to Jesus are *vaticinia post eventum* (the expression used by Strauss and Bultmann), that is to say, these are not really predictions made by Jesus before the events happened, but the interpretations placed on these events by the evangelists several decades after they had happened.[5] But although these remarks imply that the early stories in Luke's gospel are unlikely to contain much in the way of historical information, this does not question their theological value, which seems to me to be very high indeed.

It would not be an exaggeration to say that Luke, in his specific presentation of the Christian gospel, comes very close indeed to the heart of the whole matter. The opening chapters of his gospel already put the story in a setting which highlights the essential message of Christianity. That message is, I would say, the transvaluation of all values, the reversal of the commonly accepted value system. Hitherto wealth, power, privileged position have been the values for which human beings have striven and which they have respected; but henceforth these values drop to the bottom of the scale, and what has hitherto been despised is now exalted — love, meekness, humility, respect for the other. Or to put it into religious language, God has hitherto been the supreme Power, the Ruler of the world, the celestial counterpart of an earthly emperor; but henceforth God is the crucified man, bearing the sins and sufferings of the world, a God who comes in weakness and lowliness. Luke's starting-point is the child born in the stable, because there was no room in the inn (Lk. 2:7). This may be legend, but it is legend that conveys a profound theological truth.

It has often been pointed out that Luke in his gospel shows a special interest in those persons who were considered of no account in the society of his time. Tax-collectors, the sick and handicapped, non-Jews, women — these all receive attention in the pages of this gospel, even more than in other parts of the New Testament. That is why I say that Luke concentrates on that transvaluation of values which is at the centre of Christianity. This is moreover something that is closely connected with Mary as well as with Jesus, and is doubtless in part the reason for Luke's special interest in Mary.

I have already briefly mentioned the *Magnificat*, that much loved hymn which Luke places in the mouth of Mary and which serves as a kind of manifesto for the whole gospel. Whether or not it was Mary who first spoke these words is of no importance. The words certainly fit her, but equally, they fit Jesus Christ, and they fit the typical members of the early Christian communities. God had 'regarded their low estate' (1:48) and had accepted them as his new people, the new humanity created in Jesus Christ. I do not understand how anyone could say that the *Magnificat* is 'bellicose and triumphalist'[6] for it is remarkably free of any vengefulness or *ressentiment,* and is an affirmative celebration of the fact that God reverses earthly judgements of worth in order to exalt 'those of low degree' (1:52). I do not understand either how this praise of the humble and meek could be read as encouraging the subjection of women, for if humility is a characteristic of Mary, it is even more so a characteristic of Jesus Christ. She does indeed describe herself as the 'handmaid' of the Lord (1:38 and 48), and, according to Wolfhart Schlichting, this description is considered very objectionable by some feminists who declare, 'I am *not* the handmaid of the Lord!'[7] The word translated 'handmaid' is in Greek *doule,* and might be translated 'slave'. It is the feminine form of the noun *doulos,* 'slave', the word used by Paul about Jesus Christ, 'who, though he was in the form of God, did not count equality with God a thing to be grasped, but emptied himself, taking the form of a slave *(doulos)'* (Phil. 2:6–7). This point cannot be made too strongly, for the Christian commendation of humility is not addressed primarily to women but to all human beings. Its principal exemplar is not Mary but Jesus Christ himself 'who humbled himself and became obedient unto death, even death on a cross', but whose humble obedience wins for him in the transformed scale of values 'the name which is above every name' (Phil. 2:8–9). It has to be confessed, however, that after nineteen centuries the revolutionary Christian trans-valuation of all values has still not been accepted and that self-assertion is still counted a virtue, even in the churches.

We see then that quite a detailed picture of Mary can be

constructed from Luke's gospel. It is completed by a brief reference in Acts, commonly believed to be also the work of Luke. There we see Mary and the family of Jesus now firmly committed to the cause of Christian faith. After the ascension, the eleven remaining apostles return to Jerusalem and go to the upper room. 'All those with one accord devoted themselves to prayer, together with the women and Mary the mother of Jesus, and with his brothers' (Acts 1:14).

In John's gospel, Mary is never actually named, but there are several references to the 'mother of Jesus'. Like Luke's gospel, this one shows a special interest in Mary, and it preserves the tradition that as he was dying, Jesus entrusted the care of his mother to the 'beloved disciple' identified with the author of this gospel. According to a later tradition, the beloved disciple moved from Jerusalem to Ephesus, and took Mary there with him.

But first we notice that John's gospel like the others reports moments of misunderstanding between Jesus and his mother. One of these occurs very early in the gospel, and has no parallel in any of the other gospels. This was the incident of the wedding at Cana of Galilee. When the party ran out of wine, Mary reported this fact to Jesus, apparently expecting that he would do something to remedy the situation. We must remember that in John's gospel Jesus has been recognized by the disciples as the Christ from the very beginning of his ministry, and one of the common beliefs of the time was that the Christ would manifest his messiahship in miraculous deeds. Perhaps Mary shared this belief. Jesus was obviously reluctant to act, though in the original context his words did not have the brusqueness of the English translation: 'O woman, what have you to do with me? My hour has not yet come' (Jn. 2:4). He did in fact what was expected of him. The story shows that John too knew the tradition that the relation between Jesus and his mother was not 'ready made', so to speak, but had to be worked out in a growing understanding. Later we find an incident which is obviously parallel to what we have met in Mark and the other synoptists. The Jews ask: 'Is not this Jesus, the son of Joseph, whose father and mother we know? How does he now say, "I have come down from heaven?"' (Jn. 6:42). John attributes this hostile questioning to 'the Jews' in general, and he makes no suggestion (as Mark does) that the family of Jesus were involved.

The most interesting reference to Mary in John occurs at the time of the crucifixion.

> But standing by the cross of Jesus were his mother, and his mother's sister, Mary the wife of Clopas, and Mary Magdalene. When Jesus saw his mother and the disciple whom he loved standing near, he said to his mother, 'Woman, behold, your son!' Then he said to the disciple, 'Behold, your mother!' And from that hour the disciple took her to his own home (Jn 19:25–7).

Was this simply filial piety on the part of Jesus, making provision for his mother as his own life ended? In this gospel of 'signs', there is almost certainly more to the incident than that. John does not tell incidents for the sake of heaping up historical information, but for their theological significance. On this particular passage, Joseph Patsch has commented:

> Under the cross, John is not simply a private individual, he is also an apostle, a foundation-stone and a representative of the Church. What the Master says to him, he says to the whole Church.[8]

If this interpretation is correct, as it almost certainly is, then it does have important theological implications. Though the expression 'Mother of the Church' has not yet been heard and will not be heard for centuries, the idea is already there that Mary, the Mother of Jesus, is also the mother of the Church which is his body. Up till now we have been thinking of Mary chiefly in the contexts of christology and soteriology, but now we see that she belongs also to the context of ecclesiology.

There is one further passage in the New Testament sometimes supposed to refer to Mary, but it is of a different type from those which we have been considering. I mean a passage in the very middle of the last book of the New Testament, the Revelation of John. 'And a great portent appeared in heaven, a woman clothed with the sun, with the moon under her feet, and on her head a crown of twelve stars' (Rev. 12:1). This vivid picture comes from the kind of literature that we call 'apocalyptic', a literature that is full of hidden symbolism which, if one can read it, offers a commentary on the events of the time, and also a hope for the future, since it has been in times of suffering and crisis that such literature has been produced. The apocalypse of John portrays the sufferings of the Church under the Roman Empire. The woman described in our quotation above may stand for the Church or for the Virgin Mary or, more likely, for both of them. But I doubt if anything of theological importance is to be learned from an attempt to interpret this obscure symbolism, and I do not intend to become involved in it. We already have enough material derived from more secure sources.

But what do I mean when I say we have 'enough material' from our survey of the New Testament notices of Mary. Enough for what? Perhaps enough to show us that although Mary is not a prominent figure in the New Testament, she played an essential part in the drama of salvation and receives honourable mention from Matthew, Luke and John, if not from Mark. But it would not be enough to provide the data for later doctrines about Mary and it might be questioned whether it would support devotional practices directed to Mary. There is quite a wide gap between the Mary who is presented in the New Testament and the Mary of modern catholic theology and spirituality.

John Henry Newman was aware of this gap, and also aware that there are comparable gaps in other areas of Christian doctrine between New Testament teaching and the teaching of the Church today. How is this possible, if the Roman Catholic Church and some other churches are right in claiming that through the centuries they have preserved the apostolic faith? Newman's answer was to draw attention to the *development* of doctrine. Nowadays development of doctrine has become a recognized branch of theological study, but it could be claimed that Newman was the pioneer in these studies.

Truths of any depth are not conveyed instantly, but need time and study if they are to be understood and their implications opened up. This is certainly the case with truths so rich and complex as those comprised in Christian theology. But though this may be conceded, the problem is far from solved. How does one distinguish between the genuine development of a doctrine, the drawing out of truths concealed in the original, from illegitimate accretions which get added by later generations but may be quite at variance with the intention of the original affirmations from which they claim to be derived? Protestants have in fact claimed that many catholic teachings are departures from the apostolic teaching. Perhaps even strict Protestants are unable to conform altogether to the principle *sola scriptura*, for inevitably at some point of belief or practice they go beyond what is explicitly commanded or sanctioned in scripture. But certainly the whole mariological development needs some defence, if it is to be accepted as a permissible development of the New Testament witness to Mary.

In his *Essay on the Development of Christian Doctrine* Newman seeks to uncover the laws governing such development, and thus to arrive at criteria for distinguishing genuine development from mere accretion or even distortion. The first edition of this book was begun while he was still an Anglican, but the definitive version, published some thirty years later, comes from the time when he has already for a generation belonged to the Roman Catholic Church. It is not necessary for us to follow all the arguments that Newman brings forward in defence of the legitimacy of development in Marian doctrines, but we may note that he seems to assign a decisive importance to the sanctioning by the Council of Ephesus (431) of the title 'Mother of God' *(Theotokos)* to Mary. He claims that this did not mean setting up Mary as a parallel figure to Jesus Christ and therefore one who might draw devotion away from Christ, but was rather intended 'to protect the doctrine of the incarnation, and to preserve the faith of catholics from a specious humanitarianism'.[9] He also points out that what he calls 'the tone of the devotion' offered to Mary is quite different from the worship which is offered to the Holy Trinity.

What will be necessary for us is to consider some of the specific mariological dogmas and titles, to weigh up the arguments made on their behalf and the objections brought against them, and then we may be in a position to judge the validity of these developments.

Meanwhile, I think we may claim that our study of the New Testament material has been encouraging. There does exist a solid biblical basis for reflection on Mary's theological significance, and the question is how far we ought to move along these lines.

Notes

1. J. Macquarrie, *Jesus Christ in Modern Thought* (SCM Press, 1990), ch. 19.
2. ibid., ch. 3
3. Macquarrie, *Principles of Christian Theology* (SCM Press, 1977), p. 397.
4. Macquarrie, *Jesus Christ in Modern Thought* (SCM Press, 1990), pp. 93, 115–16, 393–4.
5. ibid., pp. 80–2.
6. See above, p. 16.
7. W. Schlichting, *Maria: die Mutter Jesu in Bibel, Tradition und Feminismus* (Brockhaus, 1989), p. 24.
8. J. Patsch, *Maria, die Mutter des Herrn* (Benziger Verlag, 1953), p. 205.
9. J. H. Newman, *An Essay on the Development of Christian Doctrine* (Notre Dame University Press, 1989), p. 426.

3   Immaculate Conception

It was in 1854 that Pope Pius IX took the bold step of raising belief in the Immaculate Conception of the Blessed Virgin Mary to the status of a formal dogma of the Church, that is to say, of making it a belief which is obligatory for all members of the Church to hold, or at any rate all who are in communion with the See of Rome. It was a bold step because it signalled the Pope's determined opposition to the anti-religious spirit that was sweeping across Europe at that time. The mood of the time was liberal, secularist, anti-clerical if not actually anti-Christian, so that the promulgation of this dogma was something like the waving of a red rag in front of a bull and it has often been described as a political rather than a theological act. Was it really necessary to go so far and to burden Christian faith with a new dogma which must have seemed to many people of the time to be no more than an ill-founded piece of mythology? Was it necessary to raise this new barrier between Rome and other Christian communities, including the great Orthodox Churches of the East, for none of these non-Roman Christian bodies formally subscribed to a doctrine of Immaculate Conception, even if some individuals within them did so? Even today, many people still think of Pius IX as a reactionary autocrat and see his promulgation of the dogma as primarily an act of defiance against the spirit of the age. But when we look back over the century and a half (almost) which separate us from

Ineffabilis Deus, it is not clear that the policies of Pius IX can be quite so easily criticized. The secularist forces which he opposed, stemming from the Enlightenment and reinforced by the events of 1848, had promised emancipation, but the promise was not being fulfilled and today is further from fulfilment than ever. Not freedom, but permissiveness, relativism and the general dissolution of moral and spiritual norms, has been the fate of Europe. So perhaps the bold assertion of a truth that lies beyond what can be established as empirical fact was quite appropriate in 1854.

As I have indicated, the Pontiff's action had consequences not only for the secular world but for non-Roman Christians as well. The dogma which he promulgated was not some universally accepted tenet of Christian faith, clearly founded on scripture and ancient tradition, and agreed by all Christians and by the great theologians. Certainly, it was a belief with a long history in the Church, but in the centuries before it was made a formal dogma, the belief had been the subject of much controversy. Many eminent theologians had rejected the belief. Among them was the very prince of theologians, Thomas Aquinas himself. However, when we examine what he says on the subject,[1] we see that his opposition to the doctrine was not fundamental. He did not deny the sanctification of Mary while she was still in the womb of Anna before her birth, but he did have difficulty in extending this sanctification back to the first moment of her conception. The difficulty rose from his anthropology, or understanding of what constitutes a human being. In particular there was a problem about the beginning of a human person. Thomas held — and surely he was right about this — that it is unintelligible to attribute either sin or grace to anything other than a rational creature or person, and so Mary could be sanctified only from the moment that she became a person. Thomas held that this moment, which he called 'animation' because (so it was supposed) in it the soul gets implanted in the body, is not the same as the moment of conception but comes only later. Of course, such a view also implies a dualistic anthropology, in which a human being is formed by the union of a soul with a body. Such dualism is not much in favour today, but if we reject dualism, we have also to reject the idea of a distinct moment of 'animation'. It is true, of course, that even today, in arguments over abortion, for instance, experts still take different views over the question of the 'moment' (if there is a moment) at which a human person comes into being. Is it at conception, understood as the moment at which ovum and spermatozoon fuse together to form a single cell, or is it only at the moment when the conceptus is implanted in the wall of the uterus, or is it at the (empirically undefined) moment of 'animation', or is it at some other time? I mention these matters simply to show that the objections of Thomas, as of some other theologians, to the doctrine of an Immaculate Conception had to do with technical questions of biology and anthropology and were not intended as a denial that Mary was sanctified at or near the beginning of her life. This has to be said, because some modern opponents of the doctrine, many of whom would have little sympathy with Thomistic theology in general, try to discredit the idea of Immaculate Conception by citing Thomas as one of its opponents.

The controversies I have mentioned were going on long before the promulgation of Immaculate Conception as a dogma. But controversies have continued even after 1854. Objections have come from Orthodox, Anglican and Protestant theologians. Among the Orthodox, Vladimir Lossky has written that 'the dogma of the Immaculate Conception is foreign to the Eastern tradition, which does not want to separate the Holy Virgin from the sons of Adam'.[2] But one may reply that the western tradition would be equally unwilling to throw any doubt on the fully human origins of Mary. A docetic understanding of Mary would be just as intolerable as a docetic understanding of Christ. Immaculate Conception, as I hope will become clear in what follows, does not require us to imagine some superhuman being, not belonging to the race of Adam and Eve. The danger does arise when one talks of a virginal conception or virginal birth and this is understood (or misunderstood) in a biological way. But Immaculate Conception is a very different idea from that of a virginal conception, and does not imply any separation of Mary from the human race or any break in her descent from her human ancestors. Lossky himself says that sin did in fact find no place in the Virgin, but that this was due not to some special privilege in the mode of her conception but to a purifying grace that did not impair her liberty. I do not myself see any irresoluble conflict between the doctrine of an Immaculate Conception (at least, as it will be expounded here) and the full humanity and freedom of Mary as of the same race as Eve.

Objections to the dogma of Immaculate Conception have come also from Anglicans, but many of them have objected not because they find unacceptable the essential teaching of the dogma, but because they think this traditional belief about the Virgin should have been left as something not closely defined and should not have been elevated to the status of a formal dogma. Thus, in the agreed statement on 'Authority in the Church' produced by the Anglican-Roman Catholic International Commission, we read:

> Special difficulties are created by the recent Marian dogmas, because Anglicans doubt the appropriateness or even the possibility of defining them as essential to the faith of believers'.[3]

Nothing is said against the content of the dogmas and the objection is to their dogmatic form. No doubt some

Anglicans would object to the content as well, but it is the formal objection that is more typical in Anglicanism. But while I would agree that there are dangers in trying to spell out beliefs in too great detail, especially where it is also maintained that assent to these beliefs is necessary if one is to be counted as a Christian, the trouble with Anglicans is that they have been far too vague about their beliefs, even on the most central issues. One would have more sympathy with Anglican questioning of the Marian dogmas if one saw in the Anglican communion a more sustained and conscientious effort to reach greater clarity about what constitutes the essence of Christian belief. Surely Anglicans owe this to their partners in ecumenical dialogue.

Some Protestant theologians have gone further than the Orthodox and Anglicans in their objections to Immaculate Conception and other dogmas concerning Mary. We have already noted that Karl Barth had many affirmative things to say about Mary, but he rejected the modern mariological dogmas, partly on the grounds that he considered them to be arbitrary innovations not justified by scripture, and partly on the grounds that they seemed to him to contradict the principle of *sola gratia* by allowing some part to the creature in the work of salvation.[4] Whether such charges can be sustained will be considered later.

It has become common nowadays to make a distinction between doctrines which are held to constitute the core of Christian faith, and those which are more peripheral; or, as the same idea has also been expressed, to recognize a hierarchy of Christian truths. Though attractive, this view turns out to be less helpful than it is sometimes supposed to be. It is notorious that theologians who have attempted to set out the 'essence' of Christian faith (an expression that was common in the nineteenth century) have rarely been able to agree among themselves as to what is essential and what is inessential.[5] The reason for this is that Christian faith is a unity springing from the encounter with God in Christ. Because of our limited powers of comprehension, we have to express this unitary truth in a series of doctrines, but all of these doctrines are mutually implicative or coinherent. They are not 'atomic propositions', each complete and self-contained; they belong together, so that if one is taken away, the others are affected. Nevertheless, though they are all interconnected, we can acknowledge that some have a more central position than others, or are presupposed by others. The doctrine of creation, for instance, seems to be quite central, it is clearly attested in scripture, and it is presupposed in many other Christian doctrines. We can also acknowledge that the doctrine of the triune God, though not explicity taught in scripture, belongs to the universal Christian tradition and is implicit in scripture. So we could say that the doctrines of creation and of the triune God have strong claims to be regarded as belonging to the essence of Christian truth or as standing high in the hierarchy of truths, if one prefers this way of expressing it. Any account of Christian faith which omitted these doctrines would be grossly defective, and would probably be unable to formulate other doctrines adequately.

By contrast, the dogma of the Immaculate Conception of the Blessed Virgin would seem to have a much less secure claim to be included in the fabric of Christian truth. It seems to be peripheral rather than central. It appears to stand low in the hierarchy of truth. Yet I have suggested that this grading of beliefs is not really satisfactory. Let us suppose, for instance, that in an accident a person loses an arm or an eye or perhaps a finger. The loss is not likely to be fatal, but it is still a loss and may be anything from an inconvenience to a grievous handicap. Similarly, I suppose some Christian doctrines could be lopped off as inessential, yet there would be some loss if these doctrines really belong to the complete corpus of Christian truth. What then are we to say about this particular dogma of the Immaculate Conception? What we say about it will be relevant to other Marian teachings also.

According to Ludwig Ott's manual of Catholic dogma, 'The doctrine of the Immaculate Conception is not explicitly revealed in scripture'.[6] He goes on to say that 'according to many theologians' it is implicit in a few scripture passages, beginning with the so-called *protevangelium* of Genesis in which it is predicted that the seed of Eve will bruise the serpent's head (Gn. 3:15). But it could hardly be denied that this connection is made only by a very strained and artificial exegesis, which would be rejected by almost all scholars trained in modern biblical criticism. Perhaps in retrospect the passage may be read by a Christian as the expression of a hope that would one day be fulfilled in Christ, but this is far short of taking it as a biblical sanction on which to base the dogma of Immaculate Conception. The same remark would apply in the case of other passages that have been cited as scriptural supports for the dogma. When we turn from scripture to tradition, Ott freely acknowledges that 'neither the Greek nor the Latin fathers explicitly teach the Immaculate Conception of Mary', but he claims that it is implicit in their teaching about the holiness and purity of Mary, and in the contrast which the fathers developed between the figures of Mary and Eve. It is only at a much later stage in the history of the tradition that the doctrine takes definite shape, and then, as we have noted, it became a matter of controversy. Still another argument adduced by Ott is based on reason. He expresses it in the formula: *potuit, decuit, ergo fecit,* which might be translated, 'It was possible, it was fitting, therefore it was done'. However, Ott concedes that this yields no certainty but only probability. So it seems we are being invited to accept the dogma not because there are any compelling grounds for it, but simply because in the opinion of the ecclesiastical authorities it has been judged to be 'fitting'.

We could be excused for thinking that the case for the

dogma is decidedly weak and that it would be better to leave it as just a pious opinion for those whose piety leads them in that direction. But let us persevere a little further. I think that the customary appeal to scripture, tradition and reason, while it works very well in the case of the major Christian doctrines, is not appropriate in the case of those doctrines which are said to stand lower in the hierarchy. The test for such doctrines is not to search desperately for scripture texts that might give some ambiguous support or to scour the writings of the fathers for some stray sentence that can be cited, but to consider whether the doctrine in question is encompassed within the one truth of Christianity, and this in practice means asking whether the doctrine is an implicate of those more central teachings which can be clearly founded on scripture, and which have been acknowledged in the universal or near-universal teaching of the Church. This procedure will show whether these secondary doctrines are, as Barth claimed about the Marian dogmas, innovations and falsifications, or whether they are part of the fullness of Christian truth, when we try to bring it to maximal expression. I should add that when I used the word 'implicated', I did not have in mind that they could be deduced by strict logic, but rather that they are fitting and consonant with the more central truths and help to throw fresh light on them. In some ways, theology is as much an art as a science, and its language may be poetical and imaginative as well as conceptual.

I should also add that while I have referred to the doctrines concerning Mary as 'lower in the hierarchy' and even 'secondary', I have avoided the term 'peripheral'. Mariology is so far from being peripheral that it is rather the meeting-place for a great many Christian doctrines, almost, one might say, like Crewe junction on the British railway system, the place where a great many lines meet and connections are made. Anthropology, christology, ecclesiology, hamartiology, soteriology — these are among the doctrines which all touch on mariology. If the dogma of Immaculate Conception can be commended as a legitimate item in Christian theology, this will be accomplished by showing that it is an implicate of all those other Christian truths. And this extension of Christian truth will not be a mere luxuriant outgrowth or needless embellishment which could be lopped off as superfluous, for the mariological doctrine will in turn throw new light on the truths from which it has been derived and will thereby strengthen the coherence and unity of the many elements which together constitute the Christian faith. This is one reason for believing that mariology is worthy of study and not an optional luxury, still less a distraction from the central truths of Christianity.

Sometimes we hear it said that the Marian doctrines belong to the 'poetry' of Christian faith. I said a few sentences back that the relation of these doctrines to other Christian affirmations is not to be understood as simply logical deducibility. There is no harm in acknowledging the poetic quality of the Marian doctrines provided this is not intended to suggest that they are merely figments of imagination with no claims to truth. Against that, one has to say that poetry can be just as significant a way of expressing truth as science. This in turn is to recognize that there are many kinds of language that can bring the truth before our minds, perhaps even that there are many kinds of truth. Wherever the real is uncovered and lit up for us, the event of truth takes place. Not only poetry but other forms of art as well can be powerful expressions of truth. The famous painting of Velazquez, *The Immaculate Conception*,[7] is a very good point from which to begin reflection on the meaning of the dogma, and perhaps tells us more about what it means than many a learned theological treatise. But how does one paint a conception? Something of the mysteries of election and incarnation, of deity and humanity and femininity, of eternity and hope, all converge on that canvas. The idealized but entirely human figure of the Virgin is represented in terms of the imagery of the woman in the Revelation of John, clothed with the sun and suffused with a mystic light, standing on the moon as it passes over the sleeping earth, crowned with the twelve stars — this picture takes us far beyond biological ideas and teaches a deeply metaphysical understanding of conception. It sheds its own special light on the mystery of the redemption in Christ. Later, we shall see more clearly how this comes about.

The remarks I have made so far in this chapter have been in the main of an introductory and methodological character, and it is now time to confront the dogma directly, as it was expressed in the words of the constitution, *Ineffabilis Deus:*

> *Declaramus . . . beatissimam Virginem Mariam in primo instanti suae conceptionis fuisse singulari omnipotentis Dei gratia et privilegio, intuitu meritorum Christi Jesus Salvatoris humani generis, ab omni originalis culpae labe praeservatam immunem.*[8]

'We declare . . . that the most blessed Virgin Mary in the first moment of her conception was, by the unique grace and privilege of God, in view of the merits of Jesus Christ the Saviour of the human race, preserved intact from all stain of original sin'.

The language of the constitution is that of mid-nineteenth century Catholic dogmatic theology and attempts the precise propositional kind of definition which, as I suggested above, may not be sufficiently sensitive to the symbolic and poetic elements in theological discourse. But we must pay attention not so much to the actual verbal forms as to what Bishop B.C. Butler once described as the 'governing intention', the essential meaning which the words seek to convey and which never appears apart from a form of words, but which may very well be differently expressed at different times.[9] A main difference between our thinking today and that which was current in the mid-nineteenth century would, I think, be this, that today's theologians prefer personal to impersonal categories. If we can open up more clearly the personal meanings (as I believe they are opened up, though by a different medium, in the Velazquez painting), then there is hope that the dogma of the Immaculate Conception will come alive for our minds, and in this way too its close connection with some of the most fundamental doctrines of the Christian faith will become apparent.

Let us begin with the idea of conception itself. We have already taken note that some of the early controversies and confusions over the doctrine of Immaculate Conception turned on questions about the relation of conception and animation, regarded as distinct moments in the developing life of the embryonic human being, and that even today, with all our vastly increased biological knowledge, there are different opinions — in arguments about abortion, for instance — as to when a distinctively human and personal life begins. What is important for understanding the dogma of Immaculate Conception is that we move away from any merely biological understanding of conception. Clearly, of course, Mary was conceived in the biological sense and in the normal way — there was never any suggestion of a virginal conception in her case, and I do not think that there has ever been a docetic view of Mary. But when we are considering the theological question, we are concerned not with the biology of conception, or of the several quite different ways in which conception has been understood, in ancient, medieval and modern times. The doctrine of Immaculate Conception is not focused on the biological event and is not tied to any particular theory of conception — indeed, it was the recognition of this point that led to the overcoming of some of the original difficulties with the doctrine.

For the purpose of the present discussion, I suggest that we should understand conception as 'the absolute origination of a person'. This is not a biological but a philosophical definition, and it speaks not of the fusion of cells or anything of that sort, but of the mystery of the coming into being of a human person. The definition accepts Thomas' point that only with the beginning of personal life does it make sense to talk of sin or righteousness, and it is compatible with different theories about the relation of (biological) conception and animation, if we may use the antiquated terminology.

Again, we can appreciate our debt to artists at this point, for Christian artists who have attempted to depict the Immaculate Conception have visualized it as a public or even cosmic event. It is an event involving persons, both human and divine. The conception of Mary, in this philosophical and theological sense, can be considered in three contexts: her conception in the mind of God; her conception in the people of Israel; and her conception within the marriage relationship of Joachim and Anna, as her parents have been traditionally called.

So we consider first Mary's conception in the mind of God. Here we come back to that profound metaphysical understanding of Immaculate Conception which finds expression in the painting of Velazquez. The same ideas find verbal expression in the portion of scripture which used to be read for the epistle at the Mass on the Feast of the Immaculate Conception (8 December):

The Lord possessed me in the beginning of his ways, before he made anything, from the beginning. I was set up from eternity, and of old, before the earth was made. The depths were not as yet, and I was already conceived (Prov. 8:22ff).[10]

This last sentence runs, in the Latin of the Vulgate, *ego iam concepta eram*. Originally, of course, these words were intended to refer to the divine Wisdom, metaphorically personified. Perhaps this passage was in the mind of John when he wrote his prologue to the fourth gospel. But there is this difference — the Word or Logos about which John wrote is a masculine noun, whereas Wisdom is feminine in both Hebrew and Greek (*hokhma* and *sophia*). Grammatical gender, as we have seen in an earlier chapter, is an arbitrary matter, but it is understandable that the Old Testament praise of Wisdom was felt to be peculiarly fitting to the Blessed Virgin, just as many other passages in the Old Testament that had originally nothing to do with the expectation of a messiah have come to be applied to Christ in Christian liturgy and theology.

'The depths were not as yet, and I was already conceived.' The words, when applied to Mary, are not intended to suggest any pre-existence. But her ultimate or metaphysical conception had taken place in the beginning in the salvific purposes of God. We are thinking here of the mystery of election. Already in the beginning God had elected Mary to her unique vocation in the scheme of salvation. Not only Mary originates in this divine conception. The whole human race is embraced within the divine election. This has been set forth splendidly by Karl Barth in one of the volumes of his *Church Dogmatics*.[11] God, 'in the beginning of all his works and ways' (or even, we might say, before the beginning) had conceived humanity as his covenant partner. He purposed to bring the human race not only into existence but into loving communion with himself. He purposed to do this (so it is claimed in the

Christian revelation) by himself assuming humanity and tabernacling with his people. He must then also have purposed to bring the human race to that moment in its history when it had been so cleared of sin and sanctified by grace that it would be ready to receive the gift of the incarnate divine life. That moment in the history of mankind was Mary. Even if we did not know Mary's name or anything about her history and background, we would have to posit this moment in the history of humanity, as indeed Paul does when he says of Jesus that he was 'born of a woman' and this happened in 'the fullness of the time'. As I said above, Paul needed no special historical information to write these words.[12] If one believes, as he did, that Jesus was sent by God, then there must have lived a woman through whom he was born into the world, and if one believes further that all this happened in the providence of God, then that woman must have been conceived and elected by God in the beginning as the indispensable handmaid needed to co-operate in his work. There is a sense therefore in which Mary's significance lies not in herself as an individual, but as the great moment in the history of the human spirit which Paul calls the fullness of the time. It was an Anglican theologian, William Porcher DuBose who, setting Mary in the context of the biblical history, claimed that she 'represents the highest reach, the focusing upward, as it were, of the world's susceptibility for God'.[13] Yet while Mary is celebrated as this great moment in the history of the race, we must not allow her individual faith and obedience to be simply swallowed up in her general significance for humanity. History is compounded of universal and particular together, and its concreteness depends on the particular. When we speak of God's election, we are thinking not only of the general purpose of his providence, but of his infinite care and wisdom in choosing and calling particular individuals to be the agents of his purposes. By our standards, the individuals chosen are usually weak and obscure. This was certainly true of Mary and of her Son as well — we remember the taunts of the citizens of Nazareth, 'Is not this the carpenter, the son of Mary and brother of James . . . ?' (Mk. 6:3). But if we attach any importance to the biblical and Christian account of God's dealings with humanity, it is the obscure people whom he chooses for his work. Among them, a special place belongs to Mary. We are not wrong in believing that long ages before she was conceived in the womb of Anna, Mary was ontologically conceived and sanctified in the divine purpose, so that we could also apply to her the word of the Lord which came to Jeremiah: 'before I formed you in the womb, I knew you, and before you were born, I consecrated you' (Jer. 1:5). So the first step in unpacking the idea of an Immaculate Conception is to go back to the original conception in the mind and purpose of the Eternal.

Next, we consider Mary in the context of Israel. No individual exists in a vacuum, but always in a stream of history and in a culture. It is through interaction with this background of history and culture that the individual becomes the unique person that he or she is. For Mary, this background was Israel. What did it mean to be conceived as a member of the people of Israel? We call Israel the 'chosen people', because in its own self-understanding the whole nation had been elected by God to a peculiar destiny within the broader history of humanity. According to the biblical testimony, God created the human race in his own image and gave to his human creatures an original disposition toward righteousness. The image was marred through sin, and the original righteousness for which humanity had been created was perverted through the massive distortions of human life, which persist from generation to generation and which have earned the name of 'original sin'. But the original purpose of creation could not be entirely obliterated and the human race did not fall into an utter depravity, as some theologians have mistakenly taught. Something of the original capacity for God and for righteousness survived and something of the divine grace continued to operate wherever human beings would respond to it. God was still seeking to bring human beings into that relation with himself that he had purposed, and, according to the Bible, his way of achieving his purpose was typical of him. He chose or elected or predestined a weak and obscure people, a group of wandering Semitic tribes. He bound this motley group to himself through successive covenants. He spoke his word to them through a long line of teachers and prophets. He kindled in them the thirst for righteousness and encountered them in grace and judgement. It would hardly be going too far to say that the capacity for righteousness which had survived in a sinful world and the divine grace by which that righteousness was elicited and sustained, was in a signal way concentrated in this people of Israel. As the history of the people unfolded, it became clear that its election was not a privilege but a call to servanthood. God was preparing the people for a moment when it would be ready to receive, not for itself alone but for the whole race, what Cardinal Newman called 'a higher gift than grace — God's presence and his very self and essence all divine'. Mary was that moment when the preparation was complete, conceived and brought forth as the culmination of a long history of education in the ways of God and a long expectation of a visitation from God. We could say that the sparks of righteousness and grace that had been kindled and protected in the history of Israel were now ready to burst into flame. So we note that Mary was conceived also in Israel and brought to its pitch that work of preparation which was Israel's vocation.

If the ultimate origin of a person is in God and the secondary origin of that person in a history and culture, the proximate origin is in a human family. Conceived in the mind of God, conceived in the history of Israel, Mary was also conceived in the womb of Anna. This is indeed how we most naturally think of conception. But even at this intimate family level, it is important not to think of conception only in biological terms. We may suppose that the conception of an animal may be so understood, but not the conception of a human being, for such a being has his or her proximate origin in the loving personal relation of the parents, and this love includes their longing for a child. The context of conception at the family level is therefore personal and even spiritual, certainly far more than biological.

At this point we may turn to the apocryphal *Book of James*[14] or *Protevangelium of James,* as it has also been called, though this second title risks confusion with that passage in Genesis called the *protevangelium,* already briefly discussed.[15] This non-canonical writing is perhaps as old as the middle of the second century and it is interesting that stories about Mary's background were circulating as early as that. Even if, from the point of view of a strict historian, the document must be considered as purely legendary, it presents an interesting account of the origins of Mary. The story follows a pattern that was common in the literature of Israel — the story of a pious and loving couple who have had no children and are now almost past the age for parenthood. Their longing for a child is great. Both Joachim and Anna, as they were called, were deeply grieved by their misfortune. Joachim went off into the wilderness to pray that God might yet bless them with a child. Meanwhile his wife Anna is making a similar prayer at home. Each of them was visited by an angel who gave assurance that their prayers had been granted. As Joachim returned from the country, Anna went out and met him at the gate of the city. Now we come to the interesting point, and again it is Christian art that has interpreted the story. Although we have seen that

Velazquez depicted the Immaculate Conception in high metaphysical terms as an event that takes us back to the very beginning of time, there have been other artists who have concentrated attention on the human and earthly aspects of the event and who have seized on that meeting of Joachim and Anna at the Golden Gate as the climactic moment in the story. As the couple embrace and exchange a loving look by the gate — that is the Immaculate Conception, according to some artists.[16]

Now, I do not think that they were seeking to imply that Mary was conceived without intercourse between the parents — they were not teaching a virginal birth or conception of Mary, such as the Church was eventually to teach about Mary's own child. But these artists were rightly telling us that the conception of a child is not only a physiological happening, but the personal commitment in love of the parents, and so it is the joyful meeting of Joachim and Anna at the city gate that symbolizes the beginning of the new life that would come into actual physical existence in the womb of Anna. Children, unfortunately, are sometimes conceived in drunkenness, sometimes in lust, sometimes by accident, and such children, alas, from the very moment of conception have been made victims of human sin. If we could imagine a child conceived out of pure love before God, would not such a child from the very moment of conception — I mean, conceived in the loving desire of the parents for the child even before they came together in sexual union — would not such a child be from the beginning the recipient of grace? This is no mere sentimentality but simply the recognition that human beings are personal beings, not just biological organisms, the recognition that sees the creative moment of conception, whether for good or bad, in the personal relation subsisting between the parents rather than in the biological phenomenon of a fusion of cells. Even before birth, a child is growing into relation with its mother, and from the very beginning is receiving influences that help to mould it one way or another. Already that child is becoming an individual person within the community of persons to which it belongs.

To sum up these observations, therefore, when we talk about the conception of Mary and understand this as not just her physical beginnings but her origin as a person, we understand this first as her origin in the mind and purpose of the eternal God, next her coming to be in the history of Israel as that people responded to its vocation and moved toward spiritual maturity, and lastly her origin in the loving devotion of her parents, represented in the tradition as faithful to the claims of Jewish piety. So when we read in the constitution of 1854 the words *in primo instanti suae conceptionis* ('in the first moment of her conception'), we do not understand this as the moment in which some physiological event occurred but as an extended moment which certainly includes and envelops that physiological event but embraces far more and reaches back even into the eternity of God.

After this extended discussion of the meaning of the noun 'conception', we may deal quite briefly with the adjective 'immaculate'. This introduces the topic of sin, and we must be determined to think of sin also in a personal way. So immediately we have to call into question the metaphorical notion of sin as 'stain' (*labes*), a notion which appears in the formulation of the dogma. It is true, of course, that the metaphor of stain has been used from ancient times for sin, but I think it is a misleading metaphor and perpetuates an image of sin which is sub-Christian. One might even say that the image encourages a Manichaean view of sin, as if sin were somehow a substance or something existing in its own right, as it were, rather than essentially something that is negative and parasitic. Incidentally, some such understanding of sin underlies not only the use of the word *labes* ('stain') but the adjective 'immaculate', which means literally 'unspotted'. But I think this adjective has been for so long associated with Mary's conception that one would not wish to challenge it, and in any case its specific etymological sense is no longer obtrusive. But for a variety of reasons, it is important to get away from the thought of sin as some kind of independent entity.

Among other things, when we reject the notion of sin as stain, we are also rejecting any understanding of original sin as some kind of hereditary taint, passed along in the genes, so to speak. That again would be a somewhat Manichaean view, and even so acute a theologian as Hans Küng seems to think that such a view is implied in the dogma of Immaculate Conception. He writes that this dogma has been made 'pointless' because we have turned away from 'the view of the transmission of original sin by the act of procreation'.[17] This is a quite superficial judgement, for the dogma of Mary's Immaculate Conception has a very affirmative sense and is not to be understood as just a safeguard against the infection of a hereditary stain. Though we have indeed abandoned some of the crudely mechanical and materialistic views about the transmission of original sin, no realistic theologian denies the fact that there is a human solidarity in sin and that this persists from generation to generation. The dogma of Immaculate Conception is not tied to any outmoded belief about how sin is transmitted, and does not stand cr fall with such beliefs.

What then would be a more definitely personal (and therefore more adequate) way of understanding sin? I think this is to be found in such imagery for sin as 'separation' and 'alienation'. These images get away from any hint of Manichaeism, any suggestion that sin has substantial being. Such ideas as 'separation', 'alienation', 'estrangement' are primarily negative. Sin is separation or alienation from God, and where there is alienation from God, it seems to be the case that there is usually alienation from other people and even alienation within the individual self. But if such alienation characterizes the several dimensions of human life, we can see how it perpetuates itself from generation to generation and weighs upon every individual human life. This pervading alienation is original sin, but we see that it is nothing positive in itself. It is fundamentally a lack, the lack of a right relatedness. To say this is in no way to minimize sin, for a lack or deficiency produces distortion. But the inner heart of sin, if one may so speak, is not something positive, but an emptiness. Thus, when it is claimed that Mary was conceived free from original sin, what is meant is something affirmative. We are saying that she did not lack a right relationship with God, but this expression, 'did not lack', is a double negative and therefore fully affirmative in its sense. The traditional formulation was one in which the essentially affirmative meaning was obscured by the negative form, and the negative impression was increased by the Manichaean conception of sin still lurking in the background. Thus Immaculate Conception comes to be expressed in the statement that Mary 'was preserved intact from all stain of original sin'. This is far too negative and passive a way of expressing what has to be said. The case is parallel to our talk of the 'sinlessness' of Jesus, where again we use a negative expression which obscures the tremendous affirmation that Jesus is perfectly at one with the Father. The Immaculate Conception of Mary and the Sinlessness of Jesus Christ are not negative ideas but thoroughly positive and affirmative ones.

So in our search for more personal ways of speaking, we find ourselves also moving to more affirmative ways. Instead of putting the dogma of Immaculate Conception in the negative form by stating that Mary was preserved from the stain of original sin, we may put it in an affirmative way and say she was preserved in a right relatedness to God. An equivalent affirmative expression would be to say that she was always the recipient of grace. She was surrounded with grace from her original conception in the mind of God to her actual historical conception in the love of her parents. And although this affirmative interpretation was concealed in the negative language of the traditional formulation, I think it is entirely in line with traditional catholic teaching. If we consult again Ludwig Ott's manual of dogmatics, we find him saying that 'Original sin is the deprivation of grace'.[18] Here sin appears in its essentially negative character. This sin is, according to the Council of Trent, 'the death of the soul', and the death of the soul is the absence of the true life that comes to us from God, that is to say, the absence of sanctifying grace. Mary, by contrast, was from the beginning 'endowed with grace' (*kecharitomene*) or, in the more familiar translation, 'full of grace' (Lk. 1:28). To be filled with grace is to be in the opposite condition from that of original sin. Alienation has been overcome or has never obtained, the channels from God are open, the moment is ripe for incarnation. It is the moment that Paul calls the 'fullness of the time': 'When the time had fully come, God sent forth his son, born of a woman' (Gal. 4:4).

These remarks bring us to consider now Mary's place in the central doctrines of incarnation and atonement, and so of her relation to Jesus Christ. At this point a difficulty may suggest itself. If one develops a high mariological doctrine, especially one that includes a doctrine of Immaculate Conception, is there not a danger of making Christ himself superfluous, or at least diminishing his uniquely important place in Christian faith? A few extreme feminists have in fact done this, turning Mary explicitly into a Goddess, but they do not pretend that such views still lie within the bounds of Christian theology. But leaving aside such an extreme development, we may still ask whether, if the human race could be brought in the person of Mary to the point at which original sin had lost its power, was there need of anything further? Have we not exalted Mary into the place that belongs to Jesus Christ alone, as indeed Protestant critics of what they call 'mariolatry' have consistently claimed?

There are various reponses that can be made to this criticism. But let us begin by acknowledging that the danger is a real one, and the Church has to be careful not to allow the impulses of Marian spirituality to lead us into exaggerated claims for her. I think it is possible to avoid such exaggerations, even in the case of the dogma of Immaculate Conception. Like all mariological doctrine, it can be seen and should be seen as an implicate of christology and other central doctrines of Christian faith, and is in no sense an independent glorification of the Virgin, though it certainly is an acknowledgement of the feminine contribution to the work of salvation. Let me make four brief responses to objections.

(1) To the question whether the high place given to Mary does not encroach on the place of Jesus Christ, we may first of all respond with a counter-question: Can anything less be claimed for Mary than what we have been considering in our exposition of Immaculate Conception? She was, so the Church declared, the Bearer or Mother of God (*Theotokos*) in the sense of being the Mother of the incarnate Word. Like all the other matters we have been considering, motherhood and child-bearing are to be understood in their full personal sense, and not simply as biological relationships. The mother is, in her personal relation to the child, the principal formative influence in the formation of that child's mind and character — at any rate, in the all-important early stages. To quote DuBose again, 'Christ was born not merely out of the womb but of the faith and obedience of his Virgin Mother'.[19] If Jesus Christ was to develop in a perfect filial relation to the Father, was it not necessary that his mother's relation to the heavenly Father

73

should be one constantly filled with grace, certainly not one clouded by alienation?

(2) Further, the dogma of the Immaculate Conception in its official formulation states quite explicitly that Mary's 'unique grace and privilege' in this matter (and we may understand these words as referring to her election and vocation) were granted 'in view of the merits of Jesus Christ, the Saviour of the human race'. It could not be more plainly asserted than it is here that Mary has her significance not in herself but because of her relation to Christ. The latter's saving work reaches backward in time as well as forward. So Mary is subordinate to her Son. In the language of Christian theology, she is the God-bearer, fully human; he is the God-man, fully human and fully divine.

(3) This distinction becomes clearer when we think of the different kinds of righteousness that we see in Mary and Jesus. Mary's righteousness is faithful obedience to God, summed up in her memorable words to the angel, 'Be it unto me according to thy word' (Lk. 1:38). This perfected the old righteousness of trust and obedience, developed in the people of God from Abraham onward. It heralded a continuation of that righteousness in the Church. Jesus himself fulfilled the same righteousness by his obedience even to the death of the cross, but Jesus was not just the righteous one, he was also Redeemer or Saviour. There was in him a creative, innovative righteousness that opened up new possibilities for those who became his disciples, he was the inaugurator of a new humanity. The difference I am trying to express here has, I think, been brought out well in a remarkable book by John de Satgé. He reminds us that there is an 'otherness' in Jesus. We cannot turn him into a humanistic ideal. Just as he is represented in the gospels as striding ahead of the disciples who are amazed and even afraid (Mk. 10:32), so there is something elusive in him

when we try to confine him within purely human categories.[20]

(4) The final point I want to make is in response to the charge made by Barth and others that the mariological dogmas infringe the principle of *sola gratia,* the principle that salvation is the work of divine grace alone and that there is no human co-operation with God's activity. Perhaps it should first of all be said that this principle should not be invoked in any way that would reduce the human being to the level of a mere puppet, so that he or she becomes totally passive clay in the hands of the divine Potter, but this has in fact been a constant danger in the Augustinian-Calvinist tradition, and it is a danger which Barth does not quite escape. Men and women cannot be saved from sin without their consent, and without falling into Pelagianism, we have to find room for some concept of synergism or co-operation. Now it is the human consent and co-operation with God in the work of salvation that come to expression in the career of Mary. Not for a moment can one deny (or would one want to deny) that salvation is from God and is a work of grace, but God does not force his gifts upon us and we can become his covenant partners only if we give our glad and willing assent. One could argue that the dogma of the Immaculate Conception is so far from encouraging any Pelagianism that it stands rather as a barrier in the way; for the dogma teaches that the divine grace was present from the very first (prevenient) and that Mary's place is due not to her own merit but to the gracious election and calling that look toward the incarnation of the Son. But I shall return in a later chapter to this question of the co-working of Mary and how it is related to the divine grace.

In the course of this chapter, I have attempted to defend the doctrine of an Immaculate Conception against some of the common objections. I have argued that it can be seen as an implicate of more central doctrines which are acceptable to all Christians, or almost all Christians. No doubt the dogma has sometimes been misunderstood both by those who accept it and by those who reject it. It may have been used to glorify Mary in extravagant ways, or it may have been taken in too literal a sense, so that its theological significance is missed. I have therefore tried to grasp the 'governing intention' and to express it in ways which would retain whatever has been of value in this traditional belief about Mary and to steer it away from dubious interpretations. My motivation in this has been partly ecumenical, arising from a desire to promote *rapprochement* in Anglican/Roman Catholic relations, but partly the motivation is simply an interest in mariology itself and the belief that this neglected subject can yield theological insights that are of some value. In particular, this dogma of Immaculate Conception has, I think, a special contribution to make toward a better appreciation of the place of women in the Church and of the gifts which they can bring to it.

But I end the chapter on a slightly different note, though this too is said in an ecumenical spirit of honesty and charity. While many Christians find profound truth in the dogma of Immaculate Conception, it is surely possible for someone to be a good Christian without explicitly assenting to this dogma. For many centuries, there was no such dogma. The formulation of the dogma had the advantage of making theologians think more deeply about the matters raised, but it would be disastrous if it became an instrument of exclusion.

Notes

1. Thomas Aquinas, *Summa Theologiae*, 3a, q. 27.
2. V. Lossky, *The Mystical Theology of the Eastern Church* (James Clarke, 1957), p. 140.
3. 'Authority in the Church, I', p. 20.

4. Karl Barth, *Church Dogmatics,* I/2 (T. & T. Clark, 1956), p. 138ff.
5. See Stephen Sykes, *The Identity of Christianity* (SPCK, 1984).
6. Ludwig Ott, *Fundamentals of Catholic Dogma* (Mercier Press, 1955), p. 200.
7. In the National Gallery, London.
8. Denzinger, *Enchiridion Symbolorum,* No. 1641.
9. B. C. Butler, *The Tablet,* 5 July 1975, p. 624.
10. This particular reading is no longer used on 8 December — a pity, in my view.
11. Karl Barth, *Church Dogmatics,* II/2 (T. & T. Clark, 1957).
12. See above, p. 32.
13. W. P. DuBose, *The Soteriology of the New Testament* (Macmillan, 1899), p. 176.
14. See M. R. James, *The Apocryphal New Testament* (OUP, 1953), p. 38ff.
15. See above, p. 57.
16. There is a good example by Fra Filippo dippi (1406-69) in the Ashmolean Museum, Oxford.
17. H. Küng, *On Being a Christian* (Collins, 1977), p.454.
18. L. Ott, op. cit., p. 110.
19. W. P. DuBose, op. cit., p. 172.
20. John de Satgé, *Mary and the Christian Gospel* (SPCK, 1976), pp. 50–1.

4   *Glorious Assumption*

In the expression 'Glorious Assumption' the adjective and the noun go together, traditionally and inevitably. An assumption could not be anything other than glorious, for it means a taking up from the drabness and ordinariness of earthly life into what we call 'heaven', the unimaginable glory of the divine presence in its immediacy; on the other hand, there could be no greater glory manifested in any human person than that he or she should be so taken up. According to the Old Testament, Enoch and Elijah were both taken up into heaven at the end of their earthly lives, and this was understood as a mark of signal divine favour. The stories concerning these men are legendary, but it is rather strange that the stories are not tricked out with spectacular details but are told in a laconic matter-of-fact way. In the case of Enoch, it is simply stated that 'Enoch walked with God; and he was not, for God took him' (Gn. 5:24). In the case of Elijah, we see him and his younger helper Elisha walking and conversing, aware that the end of their association was near. 'And as they still went on and talked, behold, a chariot of fire and horses of fire separated the two of them. And Elijah went up by a whirlwind into heaven' (2 Kgs. 2:11). A late Jewish tradition told also of an assumption of Moses. He is surely the most impressive figure in the history of Israel, so that of all the heroes of the

Old Testament, he would seem to be the most likely candidate for assumption. Actually, the Old Testament itself is very reticent about the end of Moses. He goes up into a mountain to view the promised land from the other side of the Jordan, but he never comes back. The record is quite enigmatic: 'So Moses the servant of the Lord died there in the land of Moab, according to the word of the Lord, and he (the Lord? or perhaps the angel of the Lord?) buried him in the valley in the land of Moab opposite Beth-peor; but no man knows the place of his burial to this day' (Dt. 34:5–6). This account in the canonical scriptures tells of a death and burial, and says nothing about an assumption, but it is, I say, enigmatic. Inevitably, the vagueness of the record about the end of Moses gave rise to curiosity about what had actually happened. Even in recent years, there has been speculation. Sigmund Freud attempted an imaginary reconstruction of events that would fit his theories of the father-child relationship, and claimed that Moses, the father-figure of the people, had eventually been murdered by his rebellious followers who then tried to suppress all memory of the terrible act.[1] But there is a much older Jewish attempt at reconstruction, the writing known as *The Assumption of Moses*, and usually dated to the first century of our era. This non-canonical writing has survived only in part, and though it appears to have told of an assumption of Moses, there is no explicit assertion of this in the work in its present condition. But it does have an interesting feature that has some theological significance. It promises that at the end of the age, expected 1750 years after the death or assumption of Moses, there would be an assumption into heaven of the entire people of Israel. The theological significance of this belief is obvious. It suggests that these ancient stories about the assumption of various specially holy persons into heaven are not to be dismissed as mere honorific legends (even if they began as such) but may be trying to say something in story form about human destiny. The stories are being told about these holy persons not just for their own sake but as oblique ways of expressing a faith or hope concerning the end of a human life that is well-pleasing to God. The persons assumed — Enoch, Elijah, Moses — could be regarded as human beings who had truly fulfilled the human destiny. In the case of Moses, he could be seen as representing the people of Israel and as already having achieved the goal that would one day be reached by the whole people.

The early Christian writer, Theophilus of Antioch, does indeed say quite clearly that God's original intention for his human creatures was that they should progress toward himself and eventually be taken up into heaven.[2] This intention, according to the theologians, had been frustrated by the fall, which entailed death as the termination of human life. In our own day, we find in Karl Rahner speculations which recall those of Theophilus. If we suppose that the human race had not fallen into sin, what would this imply about death, represented in the Bible as the punishment of sin? In Rahner's view, human life upon this earth would still come to an end, but this end would be experienced not as the dissolution and destruction of death, but as an active consummation of the whole being.[3] When we begin to think along these lines, we glimpse a possible range of meaning for the idea of assumption.

In the Christian Church, it is the assumption of the Blessed Virgin Mary that is celebrated rather than the assumptions of ancient heroes of Israel, but it is useful to remind ourselves that when mention was first made in the history of the Church of an assumption of Mary, this was not a new idea. The idea of assumption was already there in the Old Testament and Jewish tradition, even in the canonical scriptures, so it was not an innovation that had been thought up specifically for the purpose of honouring Mary. Rather, like these earlier stories of assumptions, it may have been the attempt to bring to expression truths about the nature and destiny of the human being, now placed in a Christian context.

As we approach the dogma of the Assumption, it is obvious that we face problems very similar to those we met when considering the Immaculate Conception. There is no clear scriptural foundation, so that one has to rely heavily on what one takes to be implications of doctrines that are able to claim a scriptural warrant. Again, for the first four or five centuries, there is no clear tradition of an assumption, so that one has here to rely heavily on the development of doctrine and the legitimacy of such development. But once the Immaculate Conception had been accorded the status of a dogma, it was almost inevitable that the Assumption would be placed on an equal footing. In fact, it took almost a century (a fairly short time in church history) from the promulgation of the dogma of the Immaculate Conception by Pius IX in 1854 to the promulgation of the dogma of the Assumption by Pius XII in 1950.

It will be helpful if we look more closely at the word 'assumption'. I have sometimes used as an alternative the expression 'taking up' which is the root meaning of both the Greek and Latin words translated 'assumption'. This draws our attention to the distinction between 'assumption' and 'ascension'. As a 'taking up', an assumption (in Greek, *analepsis*) is an act of God, in the performance of which the person assumed remains passive. On the other hand, an ascension (in Greek, *anabasis*) means 'going up' and is a word which gives an active role to the person who goes up. The only person who ascended to God the Father, that is to say, went up to God by right, as it were, was the divine Son, Jesus Christ. As John's gospel tells us, 'No one has ascended into heaven but he who descended from heaven, the Son of Man' (Jn. 3:13). As we shall see, the assumption of the Blessed Virgin is dependent on the ascension of Jesus

Christ; it is indeed a corollary of it because of the glorification of human nature in him. The point needs to be made because the criticism is sometimes put forward that the dogma of the Assumption is a glorification of Mary, even an apotheosis, which has the result of infringing the place that belongs to Jesus Christ alone. But, rightly understood, it is in no sense independent — as I have said, it is a corollary of Christ's ascension, and if it has been incorporated into the Church's teaching in the course of the development of doctrine, this must be because it has been believed to be an implicate of Christ's ascension. C. J. Jung, who was still alive in 1950, is said to have been overjoyed when he learned of the promulgation of the dogma of the Assumption by Pius XII because, as he believed, it brought an explicitly feminine element into the Christian understanding of God. Certainly, the dogma does more clearly recognize the important place of Mary and therefore of women in the purposes of God, but the motivation for the dogma is not an independent religious reverence for the feminine principle, but the theological recognition of Mary's role in the drama of salvation, and even more fundamentally, the change which Jesus Christ effects for the human race.

Off and on, I have been thinking about the dogma of the Assumption for more than forty years, and so the most natural way for me to expound it is to trace the stages in my own understanding of it over that period. The first time I was driven to think with any seriousness about the Assumption of the Blessed Virgin was soon after the end of World War II, when I was still serving with the British Army in North Africa. I had been granted the privilege of two weeks' leave, so that I could visit the holy places of Palestine, as the territory was then called. The actual date was March 1946, and this detail may be worth mentioning. It was not only two years before the founding of the state of Israel, so that I was among the last people to see the Holy

Land as it was in an era now passed away. It was also four years before the dogma of the Assumption was officially promulgated by the Vatican, so that at that time the belief ranked as a 'pious opinion'.

One day I was taken along with a group of other people to see the Church of the Assumption in Jerusalem, built over the tomb that is said to have received the mortal remains of our Lady. I did not know at that time that there is a rival site in Ephesus, for there are two versions of the tradition. One holds that Mary continued to live in Jerusalem during the earliest years of the Church, and that she 'fell asleep' — her death is often called a 'falling asleep' or 'dormition' — in that city after quite a short time. The other version holds that she lived for several decades after the crucifixion of Jesus, and about the time of the fall of Jerusalem she had moved to Ephesus in company with the beloved disciple, to whose care Jesus had entrusted her.[4] In this second version of the story, her death or dormition would have taken place at Ephesus. Incidentally, Ephesus was in the ancient world a great centre of goddess-worship, because there stood in the city the world-famous temple of Artemis or Diana (see Acts, ch. 19).

At any rate, I found myself in the Church of the Assumption, located not far from the city and near to the Mount of Olives. This church was for many years in dispute between Latin and Eastern Christians and finally passed to the latter. I remember it as a singularly gloomy and cavernous church, just about the last place that would make one think of a glorious assumption. Yet somehow I found myself kneeling down and praying. I did not have at that time any clear understanding of what the belief in an Assumption might mean — and perhaps I still do not understand, though I think I understand better now than I did then. But somehow I sensed that the Assumption is an authentic part of that whole fabric that we call the catholic faith and that some day I might come to understand it better.

I remember all this so clearly because among my army companions were some of a sceptical or even ribald turn of mind and they teased me (in a good-natured way) for having prayed in that church. To them, this story of an assumption of Mary into heaven was all a joke, an absurb superstition. I did not know how to answer them. Of course, even in 1946, though no one had ever been in outer space at that time, we knew what it is like — that outer space is a dark freezing trackless desolation, the very opposite of the immediate presence of God. So it was obvious to all of us that the event of the Assumption could not mean that the Virgin's body had floated off into these empty wastes. In this respect, the belief in an Assumption of Mary did not raise any problems that had not already been experienced when people reflected on what is meant by the Ascension of Jesus Christ. It would be senseless to think of it in a literal way, for it presupposes a topography of the universe that became obsolete many centuries ago. The heaven to which Jesus ascended and into which Mary was assumed is not a region in the skies, but a new level of existence. As Karl Rahner has said about the Ascension of Jesus, he did not go to a ready-made heaven that was awaiting him, rather he created heaven, understood as a nexus of personal relations.[5] The Ascension and the Assumption are celebrated as theological events, and call for understanding in theological and personal terms. Their spatial reference is metaphorical or mythological, a symbol or pictorial device for directing our minds to a human condition beyond the one which we currently know. But although I say that now, I had not thought of it in that way in 1946. Still, I was at least beginning to look for a solution of the difficulties — I believed there was something worthwhile in this ancient tradition of an Assumption, though I could not as yet see clearly what it was. But it often happens in the Christian life that one first of all believes, even if one is not entirely clear about the content of the belief, and then understanding comes later. I think this is true not only of religious belief, but that it is a general epistemological principle. Belief has an exploratory character. Beliefs are like probes which the mind sends out into areas that are still unknown, so that they are like experiments of thought. Sometimes they are unsuccessful, but sometimes they light up whole new areas. In the case of belief in the Assumption, I saw that many fellow-Christians, both eastern and western, believed and found value in their belief, and I thought it must make sense to them, or at least to some of them. We may recall some words of Anselm of Canterbury: 'I yearn to understand some measure of your truth, which my heart believes and loves. For I do not understand in order to believe, but I believe in order to understand'.[6]

Four years later, I found myself having to think seriously about the Assumption again. In 1950, Pope Pius XII, in the apostolic constitution *Munificentissimus Deus*, promulgated the Assumption of the Blessed Virgin Mary as a dogma of the Church. It was declared that

> the Immaculate Mother of God, Mary ever Virgin, on completing the course of her earthly life, was assumed body and soul to heavenly glory (*immaculatam Deiparam semper Virginem Mariam, expleto terrestris vitae cursu, fuisse corpore et anima ad caelestem gloriam assumptam*).[7]

The statement that she was assumed 'to heavenly glory' seems to make it clear that what is intended is not a place, but a condition, or, perhaps we should say, a relation or set of relations. The Assumption is a transformation of the human condition from its familiar earthly state to a new mode of being in which it enjoys an immediate relation to God. It would not be wrong to apply to this transformed condition the word 'consummation' which I used earlier in a reference to Rahner's theology of death.[8] Would not the consummation of God's purpose for his creatures be to take them up into his presence, to grant the vision of himself and communion with himself?

Going back to the document *Munificentissimus Deus*, we read there about the reason for the Assumption:

> It seems impossible that she who conceived Christ, bore him, fed him with her milk, held him in her arms and pressed him to her bosom, should after this earthly life be separated from him in either body or soul.

The closeness of Jesus and Mary, it is being asserted, could not be broken by the end of their companionship on earth. It is the fulfilment of the Lord's promise, made not just to Mary but to all his followers, that 'where I am, there you will be also' (Jn. 14:3). Here we see how the Assumption of Mary and eventually of the whole Church is a consequence or corollary of the Ascension of Jesus.

I mentioned earlier that C. J. Jung was very happy (though perhaps for the wrong reasons) about the action of the Pope in making the Assumption a formal dogma of the Church, and many people who had petitioned for this action were also happy. But it would be wrong to give the impression that there was universal rejoicing. Many other people had serious doubts about the wisdom of *Munificentissimus Deus*. I shall confine my observations to the Anglican reaction, for many Anglicans were worried by what had happened.

Some feared that the effect of making the Assumption a dogma had been to drive a new wedge between Rome and Canterbury. As had happened in the earlier case of the dogma of the Immaculate Conception, even persons who had no objection to the content of the dogma of the

Assumption were nevertheless upset by the dogmatic form. For many centuries, belief in the Assumption had been common in both east and west, but was it necessary to make it *de fide*? As I indicated in the discussion of Immaculate Conception, I have myself considerable sympathy with the point of view of those who question the wisdom of making too many and too precise dogmatic definitions. I am not defending theological haziness, which is a real danger in Anglicanism. But there is a right balance to be struck between overdetermination and underdetermination of beliefs, and there must be an area of freedom for theological criticism and speculation, otherwise the development of doctrine would come to an untimely halt. If a theological proposition is true and an integral part of Christian faith, it will eventually establish itself. Persistence, or, as Newman called it, 'chronic vigour' is one of the marks that distinguishes a genuine development of doctrine from a corruption.[9] But this development must be allowed to demonstrate itself. The process will not be helped and may even be hindered by authoritative attempts to make the belief obligatory.

There is no doubt that an affirmative attitude toward belief in the Assumption of Mary had been steadily gaining ground in the Anglican communion for a long time. In the two branches of the Anglican communion with which I am best acquainted, the Scottish and American churches, the fifteenth of August has its honoured place in the calendar. In Scotland, it has long been celebrated as the Feast of the Dormition, while in the United States it is known simply as the Feast of St Mary the Virgin and is a general feast in her honour, as indeed this date seems to have been originally. Unfortunately, the Church of England lags behind her sister churches, and makes no official provision for the day, although many parishes do in fact celebrate it. It may be noted too that the University of Oxford, with its customary indifference as to what goes on in the rest of the world, has never dropped from its calendar the recognition of the fifteenth of August as the Assumption of the Blessed Virgin Mary. Another encouragement to observance of the day will be the closer association with Europe, for Assumption Day is a public holiday in most of the common market countries. The Church of England has recently taken the half-hearted step of instituting a general feast in honour of Mary on the eighth of September, the traditional date of her Nativity.[10] So there is still quite a bit of confusion among Anglicans concerning the appropriate commemoration of the Blessed Virgin in the liturgy and what particular moments in the course of her life are to be celebrated. The confusion will no doubt be eventually resolved, and a way forward has already been opened in Scotland and the United States. The tide is flowing in what I think is the right direction, but it will flow more strongly through further growth in the understanding of Mary's place in Christian faith and devotion rather than by urging dogmatic status for belief in the Assumption. The promulgation of a dogma on papal authority is still a problem for many Anglicans as they seek closer relations with Rome, and I have little doubt that it is this issue of authority rather than any deep division over the person of Mary that makes the dogma of the Assumption controversial.

A second misgiving arose from the contention of some scholars that belief in the Assumption had its origins in the speculations of monophysite sects of the fifth and sixth centuries. This charge raises large and somewhat obscure problems of historical scholarship, and these have been very ably treated by John Saward in a learned paper.[11] Even if some monophysite influence could be demonstrated as a matter of fact, this hardly affects the status of the belief. That belief has to be judged in the light of the criteria for distinguishing legitimate developments of doctrine from corruptions, regardless of who first commended the belief. It has also to be remembered that in the present atmosphere when the several branches of the Christian Church have in a large measure turned away from polemic and are seeking to understand one another's positions with greater sympathy (a state of affairs brought about largely by advances in historical understanding) there is taking place a reassessment of the so-called 'monophysite' churches (now more often called 'non-Chalcedonian' churches) and it is no longer the case that to say something had its origins with the 'monophysites' is *ipso facto* to condemn it as error.

A third objection is that 1950 seems pretty late in the day for the discovery of a Christian dogma, or, to speak more correctly, the discovery that what had for long been rated a 'pious opinion' is no longer just an opinion but a required tenet of Christian belief. This argument is sharpened by pointing out that in the earliest centuries no Christian theologian seems to have heard of the Assumption of the Virgin. Surely the belief would have been widely known, but it seems that among orthodox writers there is no clear tradition of an Assumption until we come to the sixth century. In some ways, this objection is rather like the one already considered, namely, that the belief should not have been made a formal dogma. But there is at least a slight difference, for in the present case the objection is based on the length of time that has elapsed, together with the lack of evidence for the prevalence of the belief in the early centuries. However, I think it might be replied that the emergence of Christian dogmas has always needed time and sometimes quite a lot of time. Even such central doctrines as those of the Trinity and the Incarnation took several centuries to formulate in an adequate way and were the subject of intense controversy. If this was true in the case of these central doctrines, we should not be surprised if some that were less central, especially one so complex as the dogma of the Assumption, so dependent on and interwoven with other teachings, took an even longer time to come to full expression. Christianity is a living and growing entity with spiritual resources that may be virtually inexhaustible. Consequently its theology is also living and developing, not static and unchanging. In recognizing this, Newman showed that whatever he was, he was no reactionary. We must not be surprised if new insights and understandings come even in the twentieth and subsequent centuries — these are in fact a tribute to the vitality of the Christian faith and to the riches it contains, as well as a sign that Christian theologians have not fallen asleep in meditating on the wisdom of the past, but are still in search of truth for their times.

We go on now from the apostolic constitution of 1950 to the new atmosphere created by Vatican II a little more than a decade later. From the point of view of our present inquiry into the dogma of the Assumption, what was important in Vatican II was the new direction in mariology signalled by the use of the title 'Mother of the Church' for Mary. It was at the end of the Council's proceedings that Pope Paul VI commended this designation of Mary to the Church, but it had already appeared in the documents of the Council. To quote the words of the Decree on the Church,

> [Mary] is hailed as a pre-eminent and altogether singular member of the Church, and as the Church's model and excellent exemplar in faith and charity. Taught by the Holy Spirit, the Catholic Church honours her with filial affection and piety as a most beloved Mother.[12]

The firm bond which Vatican II made between the Church and Mary as Mother of the Church, its type, model and pre-eminent member, may now be used to go back and interpret the dogma of 1950. It will be remembered that in the constitution promulgating the dogma, a reason given for the Assumption was said to be the impossibility of supposing that Mary, who conceived Christ, bore him, gave him milk, held him and so on, could be separated from him by the termination of earthly life. Mary's solidarity with her Son, it is being claimed, is such that his Ascension implies her Assumption, so that where he is she will be also. But now we see that if Mary is on the one side inseparable from Christ, on the other side she is inseparable from the Church. But when one works out the implications of this, we see that the Church too is inseparable from Christ, that his Ascension implies the Assumption of the whole Church as well as of Mary. There is an interesting though possibly unintentional parallel here with the old legend about the assumption of Moses, for it will be remembered that in the pseudepigraphical writing in which the legend is preserved, the assumption of Moses is followed at the end of the age by the assumption of the people of Israel. Moses is a representative figure. Likewise if Mary is Mother of the Church and its pre-eminent member, her Assumption must imply the assumption of the whole Church. It is the whole Church that is the recipient of the promise, 'Where I am, there you will be also'. In saying this, we see that the dogma of the Assumption is far broader in its significance than appears at first sight. It is not just a personal dogma about Mary (though it is that) but a dogma about the Church, the whole body of the faithful of whom Mary is the type. Mary's glorious Assumption, we may say, is the first moment in the glorious assumption of the Church. Here we may recall some further words from John's gospel:

The glory which thou hast given to me, I have given to them . . . Father, I desire that they also, whom thou hast given to me, may be with me where I am, to behold my glory which thou hast given me in thy love for me before the foundation of the world (Jn. 17:22 and 24).

When we ponder the significance of the words just quoted, we see that the Feast of the Assumption must be one of the most humanistic festivals in the calendar of the Church. It is not just a celebration of Mary (though she is celebrated in it as an individual as well as a type and representative), it is at the same time a celebration of redeemed humanity. Sometimes theologians have in the name of Christianity denigrated the human race, dwelling on our sins and depravity, as if they could glorify God only by putting down man and emphasizing the infinite difference between Creator and creature. But surely that is not God's way and is contrary to his intentions as Christians have been taught to understand them. Irenaeus, in some often quoted words, declared: 'The glory of God is a man fully alive; and the life of man consists in beholding God'.[13] These words give clear expression to what we understand by 'assumption'. God created human beings in his own image that they might enjoy communion with him, he sent his eternal Son as the one who descended that he might also ascend again and bring with him the men and women whom he had gained in the world to share his glory with him. We are now coming in sight of the full scope of the dogma of the Glorious Assumption, and we can see it as one of the most hopeful and encouraging items in the Church's belief, and one that gathers up the implications of many other doctrines, christological, soteriological, anthropological and so on.

This was the kind of understanding of the Assumption to which I was coming after almost twenty years of reflection since that visit to the dismal old Church of the Assumption in Jerusalem in 1946. By 1966 I had got so far as composing a hymn to the Virgin which I entitled 'Mother of the Church'.[14] In it, I tried to set forth the various episodes in the life of our Lady as seen from the perspective of her place in the Church: The hymn began:

> Hail, blest Mary! Church's Mother,
>   Virgin Mother, full of grace!
> Mother of our elder brother,
>   Mother of our renewed race!

I pass on to the last three stanzas, where I was able to affirm belief in the Assumption in a way that had not been possible for me twenty years earlier:

> You, dear Lady, station keeping
>   At the Cross while Jesus died,
> Heard his voice amid your weeping,
>   'These your children now!' he cried.

> With apostles you were praying,
>   Saw the Church, in finest hour,
> Spirit-filled, to men displaying
>   God's regenerating power.

> Blest at last in your dormition,
>   Jesus called you to his side.
> All your labours find fruition,
>   You are crowned and glorified!

I can imagine that my poor effort at hymnody would nowadays be dismissed by the supposedly 'progressive' elements in the Church as an outmoded triumphalism. As we all know, 'triumphalism' has become a bad word, to be used in polemic, though like 'monophysitism', 'Arianism', 'Nestorianism' and other abusive epithets of the past, no one is quite clear what the term means or to whom it applies. I would like to make two responses to my imaginary objectors.

First, can we clarify the meaning of 'triumphalism' and see in what sense it is a pejorative term? If triumphalism is a pride in the human institution, an arrogant identification of the Church *in via* with the kingdom of God that is yet to come, with all the authoritarianism which attitudes like these usually bring along with them, then let us agree that triumphalism is a snare and a delusion, and we have to ask God's forgiveness for having betrayed his trust. But I do not think that triumphalism needs to mean that. I would understand 'triumphalism' as the opposite of 'defeatism', and in this sense (surely the most natural sense of the word) I would declare myself an unashamed triumphalist. For this is nothing but faith in God and in the Church as God's agent in his saving work. We say that 'we believe in one Holy Catholic and Apostolic Church', we acknowledge it to be the people of God, the body of Christ, the temple of the Holy Spirit, and we are told in the New Testament that 'the powers of death shall not prevail against it' (Mt. 16:18). In spite of all its sins and errors and deviations, the Church remains God's Church, and cannot utterly depart from him. In that sense, it is indefectible. We see in it gleams of glory that reveal to us its true nature and bring hope and promise. Not least among these gleams of glory are the saints that the Church has nurtured in all ages, even our own. Pre-eminent among these saints is the Blessed Virgin Mary. Whether or not we call it 'triumphalism', a sober hope and confidence in the Church is an essential part of the Christian's response to the calling of God. To put the matter in another way, we have to understand the Church eschatologically. Its unity, holiness, catholicity and apostolicity are evidenced only imperfectly in its historical course, and they will reach their fullness and become manifest only 'in the end' when the promises and purposes of God have reached their completion. Yet they are not just dreams for the future, not political utopias with no basis in reality. Already, in innumerable ways, in deeds of love, in moments of communion, in experiences of grace, there are flashes of the final glory to encourage the Church on its pilgrim way.

My second response depends on the first one, but also deepens our understanding of the dogma of the Assumption. It is that the Assumption is not a once-for-all event to be dated to a moment in past history, but a continuing process which is going on at this very moment. That was already implicit when we recognized that the Assumption is a 'theological event', for a theological event is not tied to a moment of time. It can take effect and be present at all times. The Assumption began when there occurred the dormition of the Blessed Virgin Mary, but it continues throughout the history of the Church and it will be complete only when the Church is fully united with its Lord, as the body with its Head, and his glory is manifest in all.

Incidentally, this means that it is of little importance whether Mary died within three years of the crucifixion and was assumed from Jerusalem, as one version of the tradition avers, or whether she lived for a great many years and accomplished her dormition at Ephesus. It is of little importance too that for about five centuries the Church was silent on this subject of the Assumption. To be concerned about such questions is to lapse into a literalist mentality which diverts our attention from the deeper meaning of the mystery of assumption. Certainly, Christians can affirm that beyond reasonable doubt at some time in the first century of our era in some Christian community in the near East, the Blessed Virgin Mary fell asleep and went to be with her Son to receive the glory he had promised to bestow on his own. That would seem to be something that can be affirmed on the basis of the New Testament, and we may say that this is the classic moment of Assumption and is worthy in itself to be celebrated. But it is the beginning of a vaster (dare we even say, cosmic or universal?) assumption. That vaster assumption is in progress now. Wherever in the Church militant here on earth there is a gleam of true glory, a faithful act of discipleship, a prayer offered in faith, a hand stretched out in love, there is assumption, human life is being lifted up to God by God. We believe too that in the Church expectant, souls are being perfected toward the day of Jesus Christ. Finally, in the Church triumphant, the work will be complete, and with Mary and all the saints, the people of God will have attained to his eternal kingdom of glory, peace and light.

In this chapter I have permitted myself a more autobiographical style than theologians normally employ. But perhaps all that any of us can do is to testify to what has been significant in his or her experience, in the hope that it may help others to find meaning in the Christian faith. I do not claim that the exposition of the Assumption given here is exhaustive or has to be followed by everyone, but it may at least be an encouragement to those who are perplexed by the dogma, to think more deeply about it. From a vague half-belief, for the most part not understood, I have come to see the dogma of the Assumption as the expression in appropriate theological symbols of some of the most hopeful affirmations of the Christian faith. Perhaps a glimpse of the same truths was present to the mind of the less than half-believing but nonetheless sensitive English poet when he penned the famous lines:[15]

> Ave Maria! 'tis the hour of prayer!
> Ave Maria! 'tis the hour of love!
> Ave Maria! May our spirits dare
> Look up to thine and to thy Son's above!
> Ave Maria!

Notes

1. See Sigmund Freud, *Moses and Monotheism* (Hogarth Press, 1939).
2. Theophilus of Antioch, *Ad Autolycum*, II, 24.
3. Karl Rahner, *On the Theology of Death* (Herder & Herder, 1961), pp. 34–5.

4. See above, p. 45.
5. See P. C. Phan, *Eternity in Time — A Study of Karl Rahner's Eschatology* (Susquehanna University Press, 1988), p. 167.
6. Anselm, *Proslogion*, ch. 2.
7. Denzinger, *Enchiridion Symbolorum*, No. 2333.
8. See above, p. 80.
9. J. H. Newman, *An Essay on the Development of Christian Doctrine* (University of Notre Dame Press, 1989), p. 203.
10. The confusion in the Anglican communion over these matters may be seen by looking at the collects assigned to the several days. In the Scottish Church, one collect serves for the Dormition, Conception and Nativity of Mary, and while it seems particularly appropriate to the Conception, has no allusion to the Dormition or Assumption: 'O Almighty God, who didst endue with singular grace the Blessed Virgin Mary, the Mother of our Lord: Vouchsafe, we beseech thee, to hallow our bodies in purity, and our souls in humility and love; through the same our Lord and Saviour, Jesus Christ. Amen'. The American Church, which observes 15 August as a general feast in honour of Mary, has a collect with a very clear allusion to the assumption, but nothing on the Conception or Nativity, so that this occasion tends in fact to be an observance of the Assumption rather than a general feast of the BVM. 'O God, you have taken to yourself the blessed Virgin Mary, mother of your incarnate Son: Grant that we, who have been redeemed by his blood, may share with her the glory of your eternal kingdom; through Jesus Christ our Lord, etc.' (This example illustrates a further confusion over the question of when to capitalize words, and when not to do so). Finally, the Church of England collect for 8 September (Nativity) perhaps comes nearest to a general collect, since it alludes clearly to the election of the BVM and somewhat less clearly to her Assumption: 'Almighty God, who chose the blessed Virgin Mary to be the mother of your only Son: grant that we who are redeemed by his blood may share with her in the glory of your eternal kingdom; through Jesus Christ our Lord, etc.'
11. John Saward, 'The Assumption' (Ecumenical Society of the Blessed Virgin Mary, 1976).
12. Walter M. Abbott, SJ ed., *The Documents of Vatican II* (Herder & Herder, 1966), p. 86.
13. Irenaeus, *Adv. haer.,* IV, 20, 7.
14. In *Holy Cross Magazine* (May, 1966), p. 23.
15. Lord Byron, *Don Juan*, Canto III, 102.

5   Mary Corredemptrix

The Latin word *'Corredemptrix'* (sometimes spelt *Co-redemptrix* by English writers or even completely anglicized as Co-redemptress) is the feminine form of the noun *Corredemptor,* so that it means a female Co-redeemer, and has been used of Mary because of her association with the Redeemer Jesus Christ in salvation. This word *Corredemptrix* is perhaps the most exalted of several honorific Latin titles that have been applied to the Blessed Virgin Mary. Others are *Mediatrix,* meaning a 'female Mediator' and this expression seems to be no less exalted than *Corredemptrix.* There are other titles such as *Auxiliatrix* and *Adjutrix,* both meaning 'helper', but these carry less weight of honour than do *Corredemptrix* and *Mediatrix,* especially when the latter is expanded to *'Mediatrix* of all graces'. Of course, it is not only Mary who is honoured by such titles, but the female sex in general, for they carry an explicit recognition of the part played by a woman in the scheme of salvation and diminish the reproach that in Christianity women have only a passive and dependent role.

In the early part of the present century, when there was a great upsurge of Marian devotion, culminating in the promulgation of the dogma of the Assumption in 1950, one heard a good deal of the terms *Corredemptrix* and *Mediatrix.* In fact, it appears that many Catholics were hoping that there would be a formal acknowledgement of Mary's co-redemptive or mediatorial participation in salvation. But that has never happened, and, as we have seen in the preceding chapter, Pope Pius XII turned his attention to the Assumption.

Since the time of Vatican II, such expressions as *Corredemptrix* and *Mediatrix* have been more rarely heard than they were in earlier years. It is well-known that at Vatican II there was a division of opinion over the way in which the Council should speak about the place of Mary in Christian faith. By a quite narrow vote, it was decided not to compose a separate document on Mary, as had been originally intended, but to include the Council's mariological teaching in a chapter of *Lumen Gentium,* the dogmatic constitution of the Church. It was freely acknowledged, of course, that there are two possible contexts for the theological consideration of Mary. She may be considered in the context of Christ's redemptive work, in which she played an indispensable part as Mother of the Redeemer. In this context, mariology may be regarded primarily as a branch of christology. On the other hand, Mary may be considered in the context of the Church, as did in fact happen. In this case, mariology is related primarily to ecclesiology, and this is equally proper, since Mary is the type of the Church and, in the Council's own words, the Church's 'pre-eminent member'. If Mary had been treated in the first of these two possible contexts, it would have been almost inevitable that the Council would have said something about the meaning of the title *Corredemptrix,* and expressed a view on its suitability or otherwise. Actually, this term does not appear at all in the Council's teaching about Mary. We do, however, find the term *Mediatrix* which seems to express a somewhat broader concept than does *Corredemptrix,* so that one could probably assume that the notion of Mary as *Corredemptrix* is included in the term *Mediatrix.* But all that is said about *'Mediatrix'* is to acknowledge that it is a legitimate expression, but one that has to be used with care so that it is understood as neither taking away from nor adding to 'the dignity and efficacy of Christ, the one Redeemer'. Clearly, any 'co-redemption' or 'mediation' in which Mary has a place is subordinate to and derivative from the redeeming work of Christ. This has always been the teaching of the Church, and from time to time it has even been felt necessary to cool down the fervour of Marian devotions when they seemed to be getting out of hand and encroaching on the centrality of the worship which is offered to the triune God alone. After the encouragement given to mariological developments by Pius XII, especially the dogma of the Assumption, it was probably believed that the development had gone far enough for the present and that other matters called more urgently for attention. Thus, although the part of *Lumen Gentium* dealing with Mary is divided into two sections which consider her respectively in relation to the redemptive work of Christ and in relation to the redeemed community of the Church, it is the latter topic which seems to be accorded greater weight. Again, although there is no actual discouragement to using the more honorific terms about Mary, and although it is clearly stated that she had an *active* and not merely passive role in the economy of salvation, the impression can hardly fail to be received that such ideas as are conveyed by words like *Corredemptrix* and *Mediatrix* have been pushed into the background.[1] It is quite possible too that the Council was soft-pedalling the importance of Mary not so much out of anxiety that Marian devotions were becoming too exuberant as out of a desire to make the Council's pronouncements as palatable as possible to the so-called 'separated brethren' of the Protestant Churches. If even a very moderate mariology were to be commended to the Protestants, then it would have to be stated in a way that would not suggest any encroachment on the unique place of Jesus Christ. But it may turn out to be very difficult to reconcile even a watered down mariology with a hardline Protestant insistence on such themes as *sola gratia* and *sola scriptura*. The present book is intended to present Mary in a way that will appeal to all Christians, but the writer is well aware of the problems. Even the very moderate claim that Mary had some *active* role in redemption threatens to rekindle the old disputes over justification and grace. Can Mary really be a centre for reconciliation and unity among Christians of different traditions, as the Ecumenical Society of the Blessed Virgin Mary has hoped? Or must she be an embarrassment who will perpetually remind Christians of some deep divisions that may never be fully healed?

We have to concede that it may have been a sound policy on the part of the Council to tone down or leave in the background some of the more exalted ways of speaking of Mary. As early as the fourth century, Bishop Epiphanius of Salamis was finding it necessary to restrain members of his flock from offering to Mary devotions which he considered were suitable only to the persons of the Trinity.[2] There have been times in the history of Christianity when Christ himself has become such a divine, exalted, numinous figure that the worshippers found him so distant that they needed a new mediator or *mediatrix* closer to their own humanity to fill the space that had opened between themselves and the original mediator. No doubt this is something that should never have happened, and the New Testament itself teaches clearly, 'There is one God, and there is one mediator between God and men, the man Christ Jesus' (1 Tim. 2:5). Not only should it not have happened, I think we can say that in fact it is not happening at the present time, because for several generations theologians have been stressing the humanity of Christ. The Christ of post-Enlightenment theology is not a distant and exalted Christ in glory but more commonly a Christ reduced to all-too-human proportions. So the need for a *mediatrix* is not likely to be felt today with the intensity that was sometimes known in the past.

However, the matter cannot be settled by pointing to the dangers of exaggeration and abuse, or by appealing to isolated texts of scripture such as the verse quoted above from 1 Timothy, or by the changing fashions in theology and spirituality, or by the desire not to say anything that might offend one's partners in ecumenical dialogue. Unthinking enthusiasts may have elevated Mary to a position of virtual equality with Christ, but this aberration is not a *necessary* consequence of recognizing that there may be a truth striving for expression in words like *Mediatrix* and *Corredemptrix*. All responsible theologians would agree that Mary's co-redemptive role is subordinate and auxiliary to the central role of Christ. But if she does have such a role, the more clearly we understand it, the better. It is a matter for theological investigation. And, like other doctrines concerning Mary, it is not only saying something about her, but something more general concerning the Church as a whole or even humanity as a whole. At this point as at others, mariology impinges on anthropology.

The general question which, as it seems to me, is raised by the specifically mariological question about the co-redemptive role of the Virgin, is that of the human role in any adequate theology of salvation. Is this human role purely a *passive* one, or is it, as Vatican II asserted about Mary, a role that is also *active?* This is where mariology threatens to revive old controversies. With Martin Luther, the principle *sola gratia.* 'by grace alone', was fundamental. Although Pelagianism, the view that the human being has in himself the resources to find the path of salvation and to progress along it, has made great inroads into all the churches in the past two hundred years, the principle 'by grace alone' has remained a shibboleth of orthodox Protestant theology. It is prominent, for instance, in the work of Karl Barth. On this view, fallen man is so disabled by sin that he is totally unable to help himself. Grace alone can redeem him, and he can contribute nothing. In some forms of this teaching, it is even believed that human beings can be saved without even knowing that salvation is taking place. It has all taken place already through the once-for-all redeeming work of Christ. It is a fact, whether anyone recognizes it or not. Karl Barth speaks in this way, though admittedly there are some ambiguities in what he says. But it is his belief that from all eternity the whole human race has been elected or predestined to salvation in Jesus Christ. This event has taken place outside of humanity, without it and even against it.[3] He says also, 'If the good shepherd (Jn. 10:11ff.) gives his life for the sheep, he does so to save the life of the sheep, but without any co-operation on their part'.[4] We may agree that the sheep do not need to co-operate or to be aware that there is any danger — the threat is an external one (perhaps a pack of wolves in the neighbourhood) and they need never know that these wolves had been around. But though this may be true of sheep and an adequate account of how sheep may be saved from physical dangers, it is not true of human beings and is a woefully inadequate view of what is required for human salvation. The salvation or redemption offered by Christianity is not from some enemy 'out there', but from the enemy within, namely, sin. It is not a physical rescue that is required — that might not demand any co-operation and the person rescued might not even be conscious of what was going on — but salvation, in the Christian sense, is very different. In this case, salvation has to be appropriated inwardly by an act of penitence (turning) and faith on the part of the person saved.

The whole question was argued thoroughly a generation ago between Barth and Bultmann, but people have short memories. Bultmann had laid stress in his writings on the 'decision of faith'. This decision is also expressed by Bultmann as 'making Christ's cross one's own', that is to say, by taking up the cross through an act of inward acceptance and appropriation. Barth strongly denied this. For him, the redemption is a purely objective act, already finished 'outside of us, without us, even against us', to recall his words already quoted and used by him in his polemic against Bultmann. Redemption is not, in his view, to be considered as an ongoing process in which we have some part, but as the once-for-all act of God long before we were born — though it is hard to know whether this act in the past is the death of Christ on Calvary or the eternal predestinating decree of God in the very beginning. But it is all complete already without us.

Now, if one conceded Barth's point, then I think one would have to say that he is indeed treating human beings like sheep or cattle or even marionettes, not as the unique beings that they are, spiritual beings made in the image of God and entrusted with a measure of freedom and responsibility. This fundamental human constitution remains, even though ravaged by sin. Human beings are still human, not mere things or animals. If Barth were correct in what he says on these matters, it would make nonsense of the struggles of history, of the training and preparation of Israel, of the very incarnation of the Word, of the redemptive mission of the Church, of the preaching of the gospel and the ministration of the sacraments. These events in time could have no real significance, for everything has been settled in advance. Human beings, on such a view, have no freedom and no responsibility. They are not beings made in the image of God with some small share in the divine creativity and rationality, they are things to be passively manipulated and pushed around. Fortunately for us — or so we are assured — we are manipulated by grace rather than by a malignant fate or blind chance, nevertheless, we are manipulated. This seems to me a degradation of the concept of humanity implicit in the biblical accounts of creation. Feuerbach's words about Luther remain, alas, true of much of the theology that stems from him and from other leading Reformers: 'The doctrine is divine but inhuman, a hymn to God but a lampoon of man'.[5] It is understandable that Feuerbach, Marx, Nietzsche and a whole galaxy of modern thinkers came to believe that Christianity alienates them from a genuine humanity.

I was careful to say that there are ambiguities in what Barth says about salvation and the human being's part (or lack of a part) in it. Though salvation is, in his view, an objective act accomplished by God, he does believe that it is important for human beings to become aware of God's redemptive work and to appropriate it in their lives — he can even at one point introduce the controversial word 'synergism' or 'co-working', though he envisages this as something which does not belong to redemption itself but is subsequent to it. I do not think, however, that his occasional modifications are sufficiently clear or that they are fully integrated into his main argument. Certainly, he never concedes what is for me a vital point — that from the very first moment when the divine grace impinges on a human life, it needs for its fruition a response, however feeble, of penitence and faith. Not for a moment is it being suggested that the human being initiates the work — the initiative belongs to God. But if it is merely outside of us, without us and even against us, then nothing worthy to be called 'salvation' can take place. There has got to be something corresponding to Mary's reported words to Gabriel: 'Behold I am the handmaid of the Lord; let it be to me according to your word' (Lk. 1:38).

The questions to which we have come are highly controversial, and yet they are so central to the place and significance of Mary that we must pursue them further.

Although we are trying to see Mary as a reconciling influence for different Christian traditions, it would be wrong to ignore the fact that she also raises issues that have been divisive, for these must be faced if any true reconciliation is ever to be achieved. In particular, we must examine more carefully the conflict that arises from the teaching about the moral and spiritual helplessness of human beings and the doctrine of justification by grace alone to which that teaching has given rise. There have been strenuous efforts in recent years to bridge the gulf that opened at the Reformation on these matters — one thinks, for instance, of Hans Küng's excellent early book, *Justification,* in which he tried to show that the teaching of the Council of Trent and that of Karl Barth on this question are not so totally opposed to each other as had been assumed: or to the Anglican-Roman Catholic International Commission's document on justification, which was another praiseworthy attempt to narrow the gap between the opposing points of view. There have also been important New Testament researches into the topics of faith, justification, grace and works.

Luther himself believed that the doctrine of *sola gratia* can be clearly derived from the New Testament, especially from the writings of Paul which had become for him a kind of canon within the canon. He was especially impressed by Paul's account in Romans of his unavailing struggles to fulfil the law, and likewise with Paul's strong opposition, expressed in Galatians, to those Judaizing elements who wished to impose some residual elements of the law of Moses on Gentile converts to Christianity. Luther saw these oppositions in extreme terms: on the one side, a harshly legalistic Judaism in which salvation was to be gained through good works performed in obedience to the law, and on the other side, Christianity as a religion of grace in which redemption has been gained for us by the cross and salvation is offered to us as a free gift, without regard to our merit or lack of merit. The recent work of such New Testament scholars as W. D. Davies and E. P. Sanders has called into question this simplistic but highly influential exegesis inherited from Luther. Davies puts the point quite mildly when he warns us that 'it is possible to make too much of the contrast between Pauline Christianity as a religion of liberty and Judaism as a religion of obedience', and he expresses the opinion that 'justification by faith is not the dominant factor in Paul's thought'.[6] These remarks have been greatly strengthened by the important studies of Sanders, who shows that in the Palestinian Judaism of Paul's time there was a stress on grace as well as works, and that Paul's own position was not so very different from that of his Jewish teachers. Sanders claims that 'the Rabbis kept the indicative and the imperative (i.e., grace and works) well balanced and in the right order'.[7]

Luther's exegesis of Romans was developed by him into a polemic against the Roman Catholic church, which he equated with legalistic Judaism and contrasted with the Reformation religion of grace. But now that the New Testament basis of his contrast between first-century Judaism and early Christianity has been placed in doubt, his application of this model to the relation between Roman Catholic and Protestant versions of Christianity must also be doubtful. It is interesting to note that Barth, in spite of his championship of grace versus good works, is careful to distance himself from Luther's misuse of Galatians, still uncritically accepted by many Protestant writers. Barth says:

> Certainly in Galatians there were and are many more things to be discovered than what Luther discovered then. Certainly there was and is much more to be said of the Roman church and Roman theology both then and since, than what the Reformers said then within the schema of

Galatians. We do not need to consider ourselves bound either in the one respect or in the other by their attitude.[8]

In theology and probably in many other subjects as well, highly onesided solutions to problems are rarely satisfactory. As far as our present problem is concerned, I believe that in any adequate theology there must be a place both for divine grace and for human effort, for divine initiative and for the human acceptance and active response. When Sanders speaks of getting these things in the right order and well balanced, I take him to mean that God's grace comes first, and presumably it is grace that evokes and enables the human response, but the priority of grace does not for a moment render the human response superfluous, or suggest that the person who is the recipient of grace is in any way delivered from the imperative to bring forth 'fruits worthy of repentance' (Lk. 3:8). It is the combination of divine grace and human response that is so admirably exemplified in Mary. She is 'highly favoured' of God (or 'full of grace' in the familiar Vulgate rendering), but she is also, in words which I earlier quoted from W. P. DuBose, the one who 'represents the highest reach, the focusing upwards, as it were, of the world's susceptibility for God'.[9] If we accept that the human being has been created by God, endowed with freedom, and made responsible for his or her own life, and even if we accept in addition that there are limits to freedom and responsibility, and especially that through the weakness of sin no human being can attain wholeness of life through effort that is unaided by divine grace — even Kant in spite of his insistence on autonomy conceded as much — yet we are still bound to say that there must be some human contribution to the work of redemption, even if it is no more than responsive and never of equal weight with the grace of God.

While the champions of *sola gratia* have concentrated

their attention on some passages of scripture and have probably interpreted even these in a onesided way, there are other passages, even in the writings of Paul, where the element of co-operation in the work of salvation seems to be clearly recognized. It is Paul who, after the magnificent hymn in praise of Christ's redeeming work, in his letter to the Philippians, goes on immediately to say to the Christian believers: 'Work out your own salvation with fear and trembling; for God is at work in you' (Phil. 2:12). The thought here seems clearly to be that God's work and man's work go on side by side in the realization of salvation. In another epistle, he writes: 'Working together with him, then, we entreat you not to accept the grace of God in vain' (2 Cor. 6:1). A straightforward interpretation of these words seems quite incompatible with any rigorous doctrine of *sola gratia*. For what does it mean 'to accept the grace of God in vain' but to fail to make any response to this grace, to refrain from any answering work? The expression 'working together with him', which has also been translated 'as co-workers with him', is in Greek *synergountes,* from which we derive the English word 'synergism', cited at an earlier stage in the discussion.[10] This word 'synergism' is the usual theological term for the point of view I have been commending, namely, that human salvation is accomplished neither by man's own unaided efforts nor by an act of God entirely outside of man, but by a synergism or co-working, in which, of course, the initiative and weight lie on the side of God, but the human contribution is also necessary and cannot be left out of account. Before we leave the New Testament on these questions, let us call to mind in addition to the Pauline material the letter of James. Luther was so unhappy with this letter that he questioned whether it should ever have been included in the canon of the New Testament. It seems inconsistent with Paul's insistence that we are justified by faith, not by works, or perhaps we should say, with Paul's view of these matters as interpreted by Luther. But one could say that the apparent tension between James and Paul should not be taken to mean that James should have been excluded from the canon, but rather that the inclusion of his letter is a much needed corrective to some of the more onesided Pauline pronouncements, as they have been commonly understood. 'What does it profit, my brethren,' asks James, 'if a man says he has faith but has not works? Can his faith save him? If a brother or sister is ill-clad and in lack of daily food, and one of you says to them, "Go in peace, be warmed and filled", without giving them the things needed for the body, what does it profit? So faith, by itself, if it has no works, is dead' (Jas. 2:14–17). Or perhaps one should say that faith, as decision, is itself the beginning of the work.

The tension between grace and works, already appearing in the New Testament, has from time to time in the Church's history flared up into theological controversy. The most famous occasion was at the end of the fourth century and the beginning of the fifth. The British monk Pelagius was teaching that the human being is free to do either good or evil, and that by the right exercise of his will, he can lead a life pleasing to God. His will may indeed be supplemented by divine grace, but Pelagius laid the stress on freedom and human decision. He was opposed by Augustine, who spent the last twenty years of his life campaigning against Pelagius and his successors. During these years of controversy, Augustine moved to ever more extreme positions, so that finally his views were just as onesided and distorted as those of Pelagius, though in the opposite direction. Augustine developed a strong doctrine of original sin, hereditarily transmitted and rendering the human being incapable of doing any good. This view had to be combined with an equally extreme doctrine of irresistible grace — though this is surely a contradiction in terms, for how could grace be forced or imposed on a person without violating his or her personhood, and so reducing the human being to a subpersonal and passive form of existence? In fact, the views of Pelagius were condemned in 416, but since there were some elements of truth in them, they continued to circulate in the teaching known as semi-Pelagianism. This certainly allowed the major role in redemption to the working of divine grace, but still denied the initiative of the divine and taught that the first step toward salvation must be taken by the human will. This semi-Pelagianism was in turn condemned by the Council of Orange in 529, but it is significant that this Council did not endorse the full Augustinian position, that is to say, the view in which the doctrines of original sin and irresistible grace were combined by invoking a more inclusive doctrine of double predestination. This extreme development seems more like fatalism than a belief in the God of Christianity. So after the Council of Orange a way still lay open between the extremes of Pelagianism and Augustinianism, a way which it is no doubt safer to call semi-Augustinianism than semi-Pelagianism, but which certainly allows for some measure of synergism. This is surely the position which is in fact held by most Christians who have thought about the matter.

Another major flare-up occurred at the time of the Reformation. We have already noted how Luther contrasted Jewish legalism with Christian freedom, and how he sought to find a parallel contrast in the opposition between Roman Catholicism and Protestantism. Calvin in the meantime developed a doctrine of double predestination no less rigorous than that of Augustine. But we do find a dissenting voice among the Reformers. Luther's friend and associate, Philip Melanchthon, was the principal theologian of the Lutheran Reformation. It is often claimed that he taught a doctrine of synergism, though some Lutherans have tried to play down this side of his teaching. But others have accused him of betraying the Lutheran cause and of subverting even the key doctrine of justification by grace alone. The truth is that Melanchthon retained a strong humanistic bias through the passionate controversial years following the Reformation, and therefore he could never feel at ease with doctrines which seemed to him to threaten such essential human characteristics as rationality, freedom and responsibility. So he was obviously unhappy with such notions as predestination and irresistible grace. He could not accept that, as he put it, 'God snatches you by some violent rapture, so that you must believe, whether you will or not'.[11] Again, he protested that the Holy Spirit does not work on a human being as on a statue, a piece of wood or a stone. The human will has its part to play in redemption, as well as the Word of God and the Spirit of God. Such teaching might seem to us to be just common sense, but in the highly charged atmosphere of Melanchthon's time, it needed courage to say such things, and it brought angry rejoinders from other Lutherans. But Melanchthon shows that even at the heart of Lutheran theology an effort was being made to find an acceptable place for synergism or co-working between God and man in the work of salvation.

Let us now come back to the consideration of Mary as *Corredemptrix*. Perhaps we do have to acknowledge that Barth and others have been correct in believing that the place given to Mary in catholic theology is a threat to the doctrine of *sola gratia,* but I think this is the case only when the doctrine of *sola gratia* is interpreted in an extreme form, when this doctrine itself becomes a threat to a genuinely personal and biblical view of the human being as made in the image of God and destined for God, a being still capable of responding to God and of serving God in the work of building up the creation. This hopeful view of the human race is personified and enshrined in Mary.

First, we have to consider Mary in the context of the

Church in which, as we have seen, she is judged to be its pre-eminent and paradigmatic member. This means that in her are concentrated those qualities which ideally belong to the whole Church but which in fact are always obscured by the sin affecting the historical Church at any given time. Life in the Church, we could say, is the continuation and strengthening of that first act of faith by which the human being responds to God's initiative, that is to say, it is the flowering of the co-working that has been present from the moment at which redemption has begun. We see the Church in its essence as not merely passive but actively co-operating with God, just as Vatican II declared about Mary. The Church in its mission, preaching and sacraments has a mediatorial function under Christy, the one ultimate Mediator. The Church itself then has its role in redemption. Luther himself was able to acknowledge this in a very vivid way when he wrote that

> as our heavenly Father has in Christ come to our aid, we ought also freely to help our neighbour, through our body and its works, and each one should become, as it were, a Christ to the other.[12]

Because Mary personifies and sums up in herself the being of the Church, she also exhibits in an exemplary way the redemptive role that belongs to the whole Church. In the glimpses of Mary that we have in the gospels, her standing at the cross beside her Son, and her prayers and intercessions with the apostles, are particularly striking ways in which Mary shared and supported the work of Christ — and even these are ways in which the Church as a whole can have a share in co-redemption. But it is Mary who has come to symbolize that perfect harmony between the divine will and the human response, so that it is she who gives meaning to the expression *Corredemptrix*.

But secondly, there is the further context in which Mary has to be considered, the context of the incarnation of the Word. In this context, the language of co-redemption is also appropriate, but in a different way, for in this regard her contribution was unique and by its very nature could not be literally shared with anyone else. We are thinking of her now not just as representative or pre-eminent member of the Church, but as *Theotokos* or Mother of God. Mary's willing acceptance of her indispensable role in that chain of events which constituted the incarnation and the redemption which it brought about, was necessary for the nurture of the Lord and for the creation of the Church itself. So Mary is not only in the Church and of the Church, she is also prior to the Church, as is implied in her title, Mother of the Church. So although Vatican II did not actually use the word *Corredemptrix,* I do not think that one could find a better explanation of the meaning of the expression than is found in the following words of the Council:

The Father of mercies willed that the consent of the predestined Mother should precede the incarnation. She gave the world that very life that renews all things, and she was enriched by God with gifts befitting such a role. Rightly, therefore, the holy fathers see her as used by God not merely in a passive way but as co-operating in the work of human salvation through free faith and obedience.[13]

The title *Corredemptrix* should not be inflated nor turned into another dogma, but it does stand for important truths concerning both Mary and all Christians.

Notes

1. See W. M. Abbott, SJ, (ed). *The Documents of Vatican II,* pp. 85–96.

2. Quoted by L. Ott, *Fundamentals of Catholic Dogma*, p. 216.
3. Karl Barth, *Rudolf Bultmann — ein Versuch ihn zu verstehen* (Zurich, 1952), p. 19.
4. Barth, *Church Dogmatics* IV/1, p. 231.
5. L. Feuerbach, *The Essence of Faith according to Luther* (Harper & Row, 1967), p. 41.
6. W. D. Davies, *Paul and Rabbinic Judaism* (SPCK, 1960), pp. 145, 222.
7. E. P. Sanders, *Paul and Palestinian Judaism* (SCM Press, 1977), p. 97.
8. Barth, *Church Dogmatics* IV/1, p. 623.
9. W. P. DuBose, *The Soteriology of the New Testament*, p. 176.
10. See above, p. 105.
11. P. Melanchthon, *Loci Communes* (OUP, 1965), p. xiii.
12. M. Luther, *Three Treatises* (Fortress Press, 1982), p. 277.
13. Abbott, *Documents,* pp. 86–7.

6   *Mary and Modernity*

Some years ago I was able to visit the famous Marian shrine of Guadalupe in Mexico. This must be one of the oldest Christian sites in the Americas, because it was in 1531 that the Blessed Virgin is said to have appeared here to an Aztec Indian named Juan Diego. An image of the Virgin was imprinted on Juan's poncho or cloak and this garment and the portrait which it bears have been preserved at the site ever since. Today the pilgrimage to Guadalupe involves no hardship, for the town is a suburb of Mexico City, included within the metropolitan limits and accessible by an easy bus-ride. I am mentioning this because what struck me most in the course of my visit was that sharp contrast between old and new, a contrast which raises questions about Mary in the modern world, even about Christianity in the modern world. These questions reflect back on the topics we have discussed in the earlier chapters of the book. Even if what was said there about Mary could be defended theologically, does it matter? Has it any relevance to the kind of world we know in the twentieth century or the fast-approaching twenty-first century? Admittedly, the shrine at Guadalupe is bustling with people — it is certainly no quiet backwater. Yet it does not seem to belong in the contemporary environment. It is not so simple as the juxtaposition of old and new. The contrast is rather between two mentalities, even two value-systems. And it is not the case that one of them has been superseded by the other. It is not even the case that they are completely in opposition. Yet one is aware of the conflict and incongruity. It is with this conflict that I shall be concerned in this final chapter. What place is there for Mary or for devotion to Mary in the modern world? But I would remind the reader that this question is only part of a larger question about the place of Christianity, perhaps even of religion generally, in the post-Enlightenment age.

But let us return to Guadalupe. It symbolizes very vividly the modern split between old and new, Christian and secular. Even the name of the town has varied as one mood or another has prevailed. Its full name is quite romantic — Ville de Guadalupe Hidalgo. But Mexico has long been torn between its Catholic heritage and leftish anti-clerical political parties, and in 1931, the fourth centenary of the apparition of the Virgin, the name was changed to something incredibly clumsy and prosaic — the town was henceforth to be called Gustavo A. Madero, after one of Mexico's innumerable revolutionary politicians. But the townspeople were unhappy with the change, and in 1971 the original name was resumed. The story is a parable of the unresolved conflict that still goes on in the minds not only of Mexicans but of western men and women generally.

A different aspect of the conflict presents itself when one goes into the splendid new basilica that has been built on the site. When I was there, a mass was going on, and I suppose there would be at least two thousand people present and apparently attending devoutly to the celebration. On the wall, high above the altar, hangs the poncho of Juan Diego, with its miraculous portrait of Mary. But what one cannot see from the church is another scene of activity which is taking place on a lower level out of sight of the congregation. Sunk behind the altar is a moving walkway, like the kind we see in airports. An unending stream of tourists is being carried along on this walkway, and as they pass behind the altar, they can look up and see on the wall

117

the picture of the Virgin. The two groups of people, the worshipping congregation and the parties of tourists, are invisible to each other and unaware of each other. The former are gazing devoutly on the consecrated Host, the latter are gawking uncomprehendingly at Juan's poncho. Again it is a parable of the split in the mentality of today's society, though what is contrasted here with the religious remnant is not the secular liberal part of the population but the restless pleasure-seekers in search of a new sensation. And there is the further contrast between the technology represented by the moving walkway and the prescientific mentality of the devout.

The shrine of the Virgin at Guadalupe certainly exposes in a dramatic way the schizophrenia of the modern world. But is it correct to speak of a split in the modern mind? Is it not rather the case that although these people are all living at the same time according to the calendar and although they are all gathered in one place, their proximity to one another is accidental and superficial at best? They are not really contemporaries. One group belongs to the modern age, the others are survivors from a past phase of culture. Thirty years ago, when I wrote several books expounding for English readers the theological views of Rudolf Bultmann and was in correspondence with him, I ventured in one of my letters to complain about what I took to be his somewhat loose use of the expression 'modern man'. Bultmann frequently talks about the modern man, meaning thereby anyone who has even in a small way acquired something of the outlook of the Enlightenment, for instance, a person who has enough of the scientific spirit to disbelieve in miracles, voices from heaven, angelic visitations, and other phenomena that were acceptable to the New Testament mentality. I complained that in an age when thousands of people go to Lourdes expecting cures, there are many 'modern men' who do not fit Bultmann's stereotype. His reply to that was brusque: 'These are not modern men!' So what are they? They live in the same world as their 'modern' fellow-men, and even if there are points at which they seem to have no contact, there are many others where they do interact. Are those worshippers in the upper part of the basilica, who are taking their worship seriously, merely ignorant survivors from a past age, unenlightened by the intellectual and social progress of the past two hundred and fifty years? Are they like the old saint whom Nietzsche's Zarathustra met in a secluded valley, and exclaimed: 'Can it indeed be possible? This old saint in his forest hath not yet heard that God is dead!'[1] Or is this much too simple an answer to the question? It may be the case that these simple worshippers, even if they are not entirely aware of what is going on, are resisting the encroachment of the modern world because they know that they possess something very precious in their tradition. They cannot prevent and may even welcome the transformation of the daily routine by technology, they are forced to accept the destruction of their environment to meet the demands of industry with its promise of rewards, their minds are besieged and infiltrated by new ideologies ranging from consumerism to Marxism. But they do not want to be wholly engulfed by it all, for there is something alien and threatening in the new ways. So the cult of Mary has continued to flourish in Guadalupe, even when it was rebaptized Gustavo A. Madero.

I said that the question of Mary's place in the modern world is one item in the more general question of the place of Christianity. The situation we see in miniature at Guadalupe reflects the split mind of western society as a whole. In the eighteenth century (roughly speaking) there took place that profound and irreversible change in western thought and culture that we call the Enlightenment. The Bible, supernaturalism, Jesus Christ as the God-man – these things that had all been for so long firm and apparently

unshakable foundations for human life were put in question
and their vulnerability exposed. New ways of thinking and
new values came crowding in. It might have seemed that the
old would be swept away completely. But it did not happen
like that. Instead, a stimulus was given for the rethinking of
Christianity, and the time since the Enlightenment to the
present has been an unprecedented era of theological
renewal and creativity.[2] Christianity has so deeply entered
into the western world that it cannot break away from it.
The baptism of Europe has in fact shown itself to be
indelible. Yet must we not say something very similar about
the Enlightenment? We cannot help being children of the
Enlightenment. The whole scientifically based structure of
modern society is based on a view of nature which excludes
that prescientific supernaturalism which was associated with
traditional Christianity. So we find ourselves living in a
schism[3] and this is not a split between one section of society
and another, but a split that is experienced in the individual
experience of thoughtful persons. They feel the continuing
power of their Christian heritage, and they want to affirm it.
But they want also to affirm the intellectual and political
values that emerged two or three hundred years ago. We
have not yet found a satisfactory way of reconciling these
conflicting loyalties. When and if we do find a way, we shall
have moved into another era, a post-modern era if you like,
when the present split will be healed.

We are claimed by two value-systems, and we have to
acknowledge that each of them has a worthy claim. They are
not just opposites, so that we could opt for the one and turn
our backs on the other. What are the Christian values? We
are bound to do an injustice to any complex system of beliefs
and loyalties if we try to summarize it briefly, whether it be
Christianity or Buddhism or Marxism or anything else of
that order. But sometimes it may be useful for limited
purposes to make use of such a summary. I would think that

Paul comes as near as it is possible to encapsulating the
Christian values in a sentence when he says, 'So faith, hope,
love abide, these three' (1 Cor. 13:13). Faith, hope, love —
these are traditionally the Christian or theological virtues. I
think it is also fair to say that Mary has been envisaged as the
personification of these virtues — and I deliberately use the
word 'envisaged' because our picture of Mary is based not
just on the few scraps of information we have about her in
the gospels but even more on the construction of her
personality by generations of devout Christians who have
concentrated upon her the most essential qualities of the
Christian life. We can see immediately the appeal of faith,
hope and love, though we are also aware at once of the
tension with what might be called 'modern virtues'. But
what could these be? It would seem to be even more difficult
to summarize 'modern virtues' than 'Christian virtues'. But I
shall make an attempt. I am writing toward the end of the
year 1989. This year has been the two hundredth anniversary
of the French Revolution, the political expression of the
Enlightenment and one of the great formative events of the
modern world. The French Revolution itself supplied the
summary of modern virtues: 'Liberty, equality, fraternity'.
This modern triad lends itself for comparison with the
Christian triad offered by Paul: 'Faith, hope, love'. And it is
clear to us at once that we are not faced with a choice
between two sets of values that are in stark opposition to one
another. We acknowledge the claim upon us of faith, hope
and love — but equally (or a little more or a little less) we
confess that liberty, equality, fraternity cannot be denied
our allegiance. Let us explore a little what these value-
systems have in common and where they differ.

When we set the two triads of values side by side, the
first contrast that may strike us is that the Christian triad has
a more personal, the secular triad a more public reference.
At the present time, many Christians, stung by taunts from

Marxists and others that Christian morality affects only private morality and has done nothing to change the social and political structures of life, have gone in search of a political theology or have tried to draw political inferences from Christian theology. But they have discovered that this is no easy task. Jesus' own teaching about the conduct of life is focused on small-scale personal relations, though his fate, especially his death on the cross, has obvious political implications. But whether we lay his crucifixion at the door of the Romans or the Jews, it would seem that his offence was not any direct political teaching on his part, but rather that the kind of person he was and his message of the kingdom of God were seen as a threat to any political system that lays claim to absolute power. Neither Jesus nor his immediate followers taught a 'political theology' but their teaching did call in question the temptations of political power. On the other side, I think Christians might well accuse Marxists of being so concerned with structures and institutions that they miss the essentially *personal* nature of human existence and underestimate the extent to which a society is shaped by persons belonging to it, and there is not a one-way traffic from structures to persons. It was in 1968 that I had an unforgettable conversation in New York with the Czech philosopher Milan Machovec. This was in the aftermath of the 'Prague spring' when, under the influence of Alexander Dubcek, an effort had been made to loosen the rigidity of the Marxist regime in Czechoslovakia. That effort was crushed by Soviet forces. The point Machovec made to me was that Marxism (and he had been himself a supporter of the regime[4]) had nothing to say in response to the personal needs of human beings. In his own vivid words, 'No Marxist I have known ever asked to have a chapter of *Das Kapital* read to him on his death-bed'. This remark, of course, ties in very closely with the phrase used by Dubcek in his attempts at reform. He said that his aim was 'socialism with a human face'. But whether anything like that is possible is doubtful. If one begins by absolutizing the state over against the person, can there finally be any possibility of a fully personal life? So maybe the Christian triad as summed up in the simple figure of Mary is not so outmoded as is thought by those whose talk is couched in the sociopolitical jargon of structures, institutions, ideologies and so on. It may be that only the subversive power of the Christian religion can humanize the political being of the state. And now that Dubcek after more than twenty years in the wilderness has become Speaker of the Czechoslovak parliament, we shall see what he can accomplish in his quest for a human face.

I think however that one of the unsolved problems of ethics is how to relate public and private morality. As Reinhold Niebuhr often pointed out,[5] the morality of groups (if it can be called morality) is generally based on self-interest, and instances of sacrifice and genuine altruism are to be found only at the level of private morality. He may have been too pessimistic, for the 'Prague autumn' of 1989 cheated the pessimism that had settled down after the 'Prague spring' of 1968. But that unexpected deliverance was due not to the state but to the personal courage and sacrifice of simple citizens. So Christians need not feel intimidated that their most highly prized virtues belong to the realm of the personal or that Mary is a very different kind of woman from the mythological figure of 'liberty' as depicted by the artists of the French Revolution. Whether one embraces the Christian or the 'modern' values, one desires to see both private and public morality flourishing. Christianity has been traditionally concerned with encouraging the personal virtues of private morality, and there is nothing to be ashamed of in this, though one must not lose sight of the question of how public life too can be given a more 'human' expression. But I do not think that the problem of public and private morality can be solved by bypassing the former and hoping that new social and political structures are enough to bring about the desired changes in human behaviour.

A second point of tension between faith, hope, love on the one side and liberty, equality, fraternity on the other is that these modern secular virtues are assertive in character whereas the Christian virtues encourage meekness and self-effacement. But this should not be understood as mere weakness. I did say earlier that in spite of the humility of Mary, she was not a doormat. On the contrary, Mary has been represented in the tradition as strong and enduring. Whether or not she composed the Magnificat (and it seems unlikely) Paul VI was correct in reading strength into it. It is the strength that belongs to an alternative set of values to those which are commonly held, the strength that can accept and persist in self-abnegation over self-assertion. In this, it is Jesus Christ himself who above all manifests the new Christian values. He is the servant who empties himself (Phil. 2:7), who teaches his disciples to reverse their judgements:

> You know that those who are supposed to rule over the Gentiles lord it over them, and their great men exercise authority over them. But it shall not be so among you; but whoever would be great among you must be your servant, and whoever would be first among you must be the slave of all (Mk. 10:42–4).

He washes the feet of his disciples, and his exaltation is the humiliation of being lifted up on the cross (Jn. 13:3ff. and 12:32). This is the true transvaluation of all values, and it brings to light a new kind of humanity which is marked not by weakness but by the strength to overcome the aggression and acquisitiveness that are engrained in human nature and are the cause of so much misery. Jesus Christ himself is the archetype of this new humanity but we see it too in Mary as she has been depicted in the tradition.

The tension I am pointing out between the Christian values and those of modernity comes out very clearly in the different vocabularies which they use. The ethical term which we hear more often than any other in modern discussion is the word 'rights'. Since the eighteenth century, there has been endless rhetoric about the 'rights' of man. This gives a very onesided view of morality in which the assertion of one's entitlements or the entitlements of the group to which one belongs gets a quite disproportionate place. There are indeed basic human rights to which men and women are entitled simply through the fact that they are rational moral beings created in the image of God. But preoccupation with rights is certainly not typical of Christian ethics. The word 'right' used as a noun denoting an entitlement occurs, as far as I can ascertain, only twice in the New Testament, and in contexts where it has nothing to do with the abstract rights that we hear about today.[6] Even in the Old Testament, there is not much about specific rights, though of course the Bible as a whole teaches care and respect for human persons. What is a common expression in both Testaments is 'righteousness' but this does not consist in the exercise of rights but in being well-pleasing in the sight of God. Another important difference of vocabulary is the frequency of the word 'sin' in the Bible, and its almost total absence from contemporary moral discourse. The acknowledgement that human life is infected by sin is, one would have thought, an essential item in any realistic description of the human condition. Preoccupation with rights coupled with a determination to ignore sin cannot form a satisfactory basis for moral reflection.

There is a third point of tension between Christianity and modernity in this matter of virtue. At first sight, it may seem to contradict my first point, which contrasted the Christian concern with personal virtue with the modern stress on public morality. In spite of this, I think it is true to say that the modern secular morality is far more individualistic than Christianity. Of the Christian triad of virtues, faith stands first. But faith is an acknowledgement of one's incompleteness. There has to be a relation to another. On the secular list, what stands first is liberty, and from the Enlightenment onward, liberty has been understood as autonomy. The individual claims the right to order his or her own life, provided the choices do not inflict damage (or too much damage) on other people.

Any study of the human being turns up paradoxes, so I suppose we need not be too surprised that in spite of the concern with public morality, sociopolitical structures and so on, there is a widespread and deep-rooted individualism. Even Marxism, though it subjects the individual human person to the machinery of the state, does not overcome individualism. Alasdair MacIntyre, in his wide-ranging critique of modern ethics, remarks that 'secreted within Marxism from the outset is a certain radical individualism'.[7] I think it is possible to say this because the collectivism of a totalitarian state is simply the aggregation of individual units. Faith, on the other hand, is an inner relatedness and interdependence. By naming faith as the first of the virtues, Christianity seeks to overcome individualism in a way more radical than anything that we find in secular morality.

Is there a point of convergence between the two sets of values set up by love on the Christian side and fraternity on the secular side? Both are commending the solidarity of human beings, yet there are differences even here. Christian love, which may be denoted by special words such as the Greek *agape* or the Latin *caritas,* is sometimes held to be quite unique. Its difference from some other forms of love (and the word 'love', it must be acknowledged, is a very indefinite and much abused term) cannot be doubted, but sometimes the differences are exaggerated. Among the characteristics of Christian love may be mentioned: its universal or non-discriminating character — like God's own love for his creatures, Christian love should be open to anyone who stands in need of the loving action; its non-sentimental character — the fact that the Christian is *commanded* to love shows that this love is not a passion or involuntary emotion, but a chosen attitude toward the other, the attitude which may be described as 'letting-be'; but one has to add a third character — though not an emotion, Christian love is equally not a clinical beneficence but includes compassion, the sense of an inner bond to the other as a child of God. The idea of fraternity has much in common with this Christian idea of love — indeed, some theologians (Harnack is an example) have freely used the term 'brotherhood' for the theological conception of human solidarity under God. (Incidentally, it seems to be difficult to find in English or other languages an alternative expression to 'fraternity' or 'brotherhood' that would explicitly include women, though of course they are implicitly included in the 'fraternal' community.) But the word 'fraternity' cannot quite divest itself of the associations of kinship and common interest that originally attach to it, and thus it never attains that non-discriminating universality attendant on the Christian understanding of love, and in any case a secular ideal is bound to lack the concrete archetype of God's own love which is the ultimate source of the Christian idea.

However, I do not wish to get involved here in arguments over the relative merits and demerits of religious and secular moralities.[8] I have acknowledged that the modern man or woman may well be attracted both by the traditional Christian values and by the serious moral and political values of the post-Enlightenment era, and I have argued that although there is no obvious or easy way in which these can be combined, it would be a mistake for the secular mind to discard the Christian values, just as it would also be a mistake if the Christian did not struggle with the question of how the values derived from the New Testament can be made effective in the vastly more complicated world of our own time. In particular, we have been thinking of Mary who, as the pre-eminent member of the Church, embodies these values. How are we to think of her in the present-day context? I do not think that we can or should attempt to modernize her. It is not convincing to make a somewhat dubious appeal to the Magnificat, let us say, and to present Mary as a champion of liberation or emancipation. Apart from the fact that such a presentation would be historically untrue, it would also be untrue to the integrity of Mary herself. She has that integrity in her own time and context, solidly founded on those Christian values which, as I have tried to show, are certainly not inferior to the values of the modern world. Mary will not be made relevant by making her fit into our modern patterns, but rather by seeing her as a sign of contradiction. She contradicts the neglect of the personal, the assertiveness and the individualism of the modern world. I said that it is not easy to combine the Christian heritage with whatever is of value in the modern mentality. But if we cannot combine them, we must endeavour to hold them together in their provisional contradictoriness, so that each may correct and eventually enrich the other. That helps to explain why a modern devotion to Mary will be in many ways different from a medieval devotion. We are bound to relate to her in a way that recognizes not only her affirmative qualities but the tension between these and the values of today.

I do not say it will clarify these matters for us, but it will help us to see something of their far-reaching ramifications if we turn now to a comparison of two women — Mary, the

Mother of the Lord, and Margarete, the heroine of Goethe's *Faust*. Part 1 of that famous drama was published in 1808, Part 2 was completed shortly before Goethe's death in 1832. The total length of time spent on its composition is said to have been sixty years. It stands, of course, as one of the half dozen or so greatest literary productions of the human mind, and it touches closely at many points on our own theme. Many people know at least the famous closing chorus:

Das ewig weibliche zieht uns heran (The eternal feminine draws us on).

The words remind us of the starting-point of this book — the so-called 'sexual revolution', the drive for greater freedom, dignity and influence for women, and our specific question about the significance of the Blessed Virgin Mary for these developments.

There was a real Faust who died about 1540. He dabbled in science and had a reputation as a magician. Curiously, he seems to have been admired by Luther and Melanchthon, but generally he was feared and was supposed to have sold his soul to the devil in exchange for his occult knowledge. One can see how this legend would appeal to the minds of the Renaissance and Enlightenment and one of the great Enlightenment thinkers, Lessing, did in fact rehabilitate the figure of Faust, praising his quest for knowledge and representing him as finally reconciled to God. In Goethe's drama, Faust has the characteristics of the western man who, like Goethe himself, has known the Enlightenment and the Romantic reaction. We can see in Faust the tensions and contradictions which I mentioned in describing the Marian shrine at Guadalupe, tensions which we today still know in ourselves and have not been able to resolve. So

Faust says of himself:

> Two souls, alas! reside within my breast,
> And each is eager for a separation. (1112–13)[9]

He is on the one hand irreligious, and Margarete complains about this. Yet he has his own pantheistic religiosity and does not believe that knowledge alone can bring salvation:

> I do not seek salvation in mere apathy.
> Awe is the greatest boon we humans are allotted,
> And though our world would have us stifle feeling,
> If we are stirred profoundly, we sense the Infinite
> (6271–4)

But this God (like Schleiermacher's Infinite?) is more of a vague sentiment than a clear belief, and has no clearly Christian content:

> Who can name him?
> I have no name to give it.
> Feeling is everything.

But such a vague quasi-romantic religion tends to lapse into materialism as scientific knowledge and power increase. A parable of the modern world?

> When we attain this world's material goods,
> All better things are called a madman's fancies. (636–7)

Yet there remains something uncorrupted in Faust, something authentically human. He struggles (though not very firmly) against Mephistopheles' schemes for the seduction of Margarete, and even calls him a 'perfidious,

contemptible spirit'. Mephisotopheles for his part re-
proaches Faust for having made a contract, the terms of
which he is unable or unwilling to keep.

Margarete or Gretchen shows also a split mind, though
the tensions here are different from what we saw in Faust.
Margarete is a Christian believer and observant of her
religious duties. She is upset by Faust's apparent
indifference, and also worried about the influence which
Mephistopheles has over him. But Gretchen is no paragon
of virtue. When Mephistopheles hides some jewellery in her
cottage, her acquisitive instinct is easily roused. Again, she
offers no resistance to the advances of Faust. Gretchen is
cast more in the mould of Mary Magdalen, the penitent
sinner, than of Mary Immaculate, in whom grace was
triumphant from the beginning. We live, however, in an age
of levelling down, an age which resents the exceptional man
or woman and proceeds at once to look for flaws and is
unhappy if none are to be found. How many biographies
nowadays win notoriety for their authors by debunking some
hero or heroine of the past. So today some people do declare
a preference for Mary of Magdala over Mary of Nazareth.
Marina Warner, for instance, in a book significantly entitled
Alone of All Her Sex', writes:

> The Virgin's unspotted goodness prevents the sinner from
> identifying with her, and keeps her in the position of the
> Platonic ideal; but Mary Magdalene holds up a comforting
> mirror to those who sin again and again, and promises joy
> to human frailty.[10]

But to this it may be replied that perhaps we must look
ultimately to the Platonic ideal for a challenge and
inspiration not to be found elsewhere.

But in the end it is not Gretchen's moral lapses that
contrast her with the Virgin but the inferior kind of love,

namely, romantic love, that she represents and that the word 'love' most commonly suggests in the modern western world. Goethe does indeed declare:

It is all-potent love that gives
All things their form, sustains all things. (11872–3).

At the very end of the drama, the Virgin herself appears, under the description *Mater gloriosa*. Gretchen is now in company with three penitent women, Mary Magdalen, the Samaritan woman of John's gospel and Mary of Egypt, a semi-legendary courtesan who is said to have converted to Christianity in the fifth century. To them the Virgin calls:

Come, rise to higher spheres.
Seeing your presence, he will follow'. (12094–5).

The last line quoted here refers of course to Faust — he follows the 'eternal feminine' and finally (according to the usual interpretation) attains salvation. A commentator on *Faust,* O. Durrani, makes a just comment:

The Virgin would have to be presented not as an emblem of femininity or maternity as such, but primarily as the Mother of the Saviour. However, the main function that she has in Christian thought is glossed over in *Faust* and the play reaches its conclusion with that strange combination of religious mystique and secular emotionalism which enables the all-too-human to be raised to the level of a natural theology.[11]

The only comment I would add to this is that it is a very poor and thin natural theology that we encounter here.

One further question remains to be considered. Our concern up to this point has been chiefly with the place of

Mary in Christian belief and its significance for the place of women in the Church and in society generally. We now have to ask the practical question of how the theological significance of Mary is to be appropriated in worship and spirituality. This is the question of Marian devotions, and admittedly it is a controversial one. So perhaps I should state right away a fundamental principle that has always been acknowledged in the Church, though it may sometimes have been obscured — that all our devotion, including any that has been inspired by Mary, is ultimately devotion to God in Christ. There have been few devotees of Mary so enthusiastic as Louis de Montfort, whose book on devotion to Mary is still widely used. But no one could be more forthright in making it clear that devotion to Mary is not an end in itself or an independent cult. He writes:

> I avow, with all the Church, that Mary, being a mere creature that has come from the hands of the most High, is in comparison with his infinite majesty less than an atom; or rather, she is nothing at all, because only he is He Who Is . . . Jesus Christ, our Saviour, true God and true Man, ought to be the last end of all our devotions, else they are false and delusive. If then we establish solid devotion to our blessed Lady, it is only more perfectly to establish devotion to Christ . . . When we praise her, love her, honour her or give anything to her, it is God who is praised, God who is loved, God who is glorified and it is to God that we give, through Mary and in Mary.[12]

Mary appears frequently in the public liturgy of the Church, both in feasts which commemorate events in her own career, such as the Annunciation, and in other feasts such as Christmas, where Mary, though not at the centre, is very much present. On these liturgical occasions, there is no danger of any distortion or exaggeration, because Mary is presented within the wider context of Christian faith and in the course of an act of worship directed toward God. But many Christians supplement the occasions of public worship by private devotions, and Mary features in these also. In the churches of both east and west, Mary is celebrated in special hymns, prayers, offices, even pilgrimages. The tendency at the present time is to keep these simple and restrained, and this is how they are most likely to establish themselves ecumenically, even among Christians whose traditions have not in the past provided for any Marian devotions. Readers will find an ecumenical office provided in this book.[13] Pope Paul VI specially commended two of the simplest acts of devotion to Mary — the Angelus and the Rosary. The first of these is a calling to mind of the angel's announcement to Mary, of Mary's acceptance of her vocation, and of the incarnation. The second has been described as a 'compendium of the gospel'. They are both meditative acts in which our minds dwell on high moments in the history of salvation and we share in the communion of saints and are strengthened by them.

Notes

1. F. W. Nietzsche, *Thus Spake Zarathustra* (Dent, 1933), p. 5.
2. See J. Macquarrie, *Jesus Christ in Modern Thought* (SCM Press, 1990), Part 2.
3. See Martin E. Marty, *The Modern Schism* (Harper & Row, 1969).
4. See M. Machovec, *A Marxist Looks at Jesus* (Darton, Longman & Todd, 1976).
5. See, e.g., Reinhold Niebuhr, *Man's Nature and his Communities* (Scribner, 1965).
6. Heb. 13:10 and Rev. 22:14.
7. A. MacIntyre, *After Virtue* (University of Notre Dame Press, 1984), p. 261.
8. See Basil Mitchell, *Morality, Religious and Secular* (OUP, 1980).
9. Quotations are from the translation by Stuart Atkins, *Faust 1 & 2* (Suhrkamp, 1984). Figures in brackets refer to the lines of the drama.

10. M. Warner, *Alone of All Her Sex* (Weidenfeld & Nicholson, 1976), p. 235.
11. O. Durrani, *Faust and the Bible* (Peter Lang, 1977), p. 173.
12. Louis de Montfort, *True Devotion to Mary* (Tan Books, 1985), pp. 11, 37–8, 105.
13. See below, p. 139.

Part Two

An Ecumenical Office of Mary the Mother of Jesus

General Notes

a) The Office of the Ecumenical Society of the Blessed Virgin Mary arose as an attempt by the compiler to build some basic devotions around a commonly accepted version of the Magnificat. Prior to 1981 gatherings of the Society found it impossible to recite a common version of the Song of Mary without a printed text before them. Since 1981 the original office has been reprinted many times and has become part of the life blood of the Society. With the exception of a different hymn in the office and the placing of the Ven. George Timm's hymn in an appendix, the office is original 1981 material, copyright the ESBVM. The appendices are new. An additional appendix of hymns is only included in the full version of the Office available from the Society.

b) This act of worship corresponds to the ancient Little Office of the Blessed Virgin. Hence, although it includes the Magnificat, it is not particularly an evening office, and can be used at any time of day.

c) The office may be led throughout by a lay person.

d) The *ICET* version of the Magnificat is an agreed text for Roman Catholics, Anglicans and members of the Free Churches.

Norman Wallwork, Liturgy Secretary
Ecumenical Society of the Blessed Virgin Mary
11 Belmont Road, Wallington, Surrey
Feast of the Annunciation 1990

1 INVOCATION

In the name of the Father, and of the Son,
and of the Holy Spirit. **Amen.**

2 SCRIPTURE SENTENCE

This or some other sentence of scripture:

A virgin shall conceive and bear a son, and his name
shall be called Emmanuel.   *Isaiah 7:14*

3 ACT OF PENITENCE

Let us confess our sins to almighty God.

A short silence
This or some other prayer of confession:

We confess to almighty God,
before blessed Mary,
before the holy Apostles,
and all the company of heaven,
that we have sinned
through our own fault
in our thoughts and in our words,
in what we have done,
and in what we have failed to do;
we pray almighty God to have mercy on us.

4 PRAYER FOR FORGIVENESS

This or some other prayer:

The almighty and merciful Lord
grant us pardon and forgiveness,
the absolution and remission of our sins,
time for amendment of life,
and the grace and comfort of the Holy Spirit. **Amen.**

5 VERSICLES AND RESPONSES

Our help is in the name of the Lord:
who has made heaven and earth.

O God, make speed to save us:
O Lord, make haste to help us.

Glory to the Father, and to the Son,
and to the Holy Spirit:
**as it was in the beginning, is now,
and shall be for ever. Amen.**

6 THE OFFICE HYMN

This or some other hymn:

For Mary, Mother of the Lord,
God's holy name be praised,
Who first the Son of God adored
As on her child she gazed.

The angel Gabriel brought the word
She should Christ's mother be;
Our Lady, handmaid of the Lord,
Made answer willingly.

The heavenly call she thus obeyed,
And so God's will was done;
The second Eve love's answer made
Which our redemption won.

She gave her body for God's shrine,
Her heart to piercing pain,
And knew the cost of love divine
When Jesus Christ was slain.

Dear Mary, from your lowliness
And home in Galilee,
There comes a joy and holiness
To every family.

Hail, Mary, you are full of grace,
Above all women blest;
Blest in your Son, whom your embrace
In birth and death confessed.

J. R. Peacey

Sit

7   THE PSALM

This or some other psalm:

PSALM 112 (113)

The Lord raises up the lowly
The Lord lifts up the poor.

O sing praises you that are his servants:
O praise the name of the Lord.

Let the name of the Lord be blessed:
from this time forward and for ever.

From the rising of the sun to its going down:
let the name of the Lord be praised.

The Lord is exalted over all the nations:
and his glory is above the heavens.

Who can be likened to the Lord our God:
in heaven or upon the earth,

Who has his dwellings so high:
yet condescends to look on things beneath?

He raises the lowly from the dust:
and lifts up the poor from their misery;

He gives them a place among the princes:
even among the princes of his people.

He causes the barren woman to keep house:
and makes her a joyful mother of children.

Glory to the Father, and to the Son,
and to the Holy Spirit:
as it was in the beginning, is now,
and shall be for ever. Amen.

The Lord raises up the lowly:
The Lord lifts up the poor.

8   THE CANTICLE

This or some other canticle:

BLESS THE LORD

The Holy Spirit will come upon you:
and the power of the Most High will overshadow you.

Bless the Lord, the God of our fathers:
bless his holy and glorious name.

Bless him in his holy and glorious temple:
sing his praise and exalt him for ever.

Bless him who beholds the depths:
bless him who sits between the cherubim.

Bless him on the throne of his kingdom:
sing his praise and exalt him for ever.

Bless him in the heights of heaven:
sing his praise and exalt him for ever.

Bless the Father, the Son, and the Holy Spirit:
sing his praise and exalt him for ever.

The Holy Spirit will come upon you:
and the power of the Most High will overshadow you.

9   THE LESSON AND RESPONSORY

This or some other passage of scripture:

When the time had fully come, God sent forth his
Son, born of a woman, born under the law, to
redeem those who were under the law, so that we
might receive adoption as sons.

Galatians 4:4 and 5

Behold I am the handmaid of the Lord:
let it be to me according to your word.
Behold I am the handmaid of the Lord:
let it be to me according to your word.

I have come to do your will, O God.
Behold I am the handmaid of the Lord:
let it be to me according to your word.

Glory to the Father, and to the Son,
and to the Holy Spirit:
Behold I am the handmaid of the Lord:
let it be to me according to your word.

Stand

10   THE MAGNIFICAT   The Song of Mary

Blessed are you among women:
and blessed is the fruit of your womb!

My soul proclaims the greatness of the Lord:
my spirit rejoices in God my Saviour;

for he has looked with favour on his lowly servant:
from this day all generations will call me blessed;

the Almight has done great things for me:
and holy is his name.

He has mercy on those who fear him:
in every generation.

He has shown the strength of his arm:
he has scattered the proud in their conceit.

He has cast down the mighty from their thrones:
and has lifted up the lowly.

He has filled the hungry with good things:
and the rich he has sent away empty.

He has come to the help of his servant Israel;
for he has remembered his promise of mercy,

the promise he made to our fathers:
to Abraham and his children for ever.

Glory to the Father, and to the Son,
and to the Holy Spirit:
as it was in the beginning, is now,
and shall be for ever. Amen.

Blessed are you among women:
and blessed is the fruit of your womb!

11 THANKSGIVING

This or some other act of thanksgiving:

In the joy of creation:
Blessed be God.

In the presence of Christ:
Blessed be God.

In the power of the Spirit:
Blessed be God.

In the Mother of Jesus:
Blessed be God.

In his martyrs and saints:
Blessed be God.

In his glorious gospel:
Blessed be God.

In his holy Church:
Blessed be God.

In the Waters of Baptism:
Blessed be God.

In the Bread of Angels:
Blessed be God.

In time and eternity:
Blessed be God.

12   INTERCESSIONS

This or some other act of intercession:

For the coming of the Kingdom:
We pray to the Lord.

For the unity of the Church:
We pray to the Lord.

For the peace of the world:
We pray to the Lord.

For the suffering and the sorrowful:
We pray to the Lord.

For the faithful departed:
We pray to the Lord.

13   THE LORD'S PRAYER

As our Saviour has taught us, so we pray.

**Our Father, who art in heaven,
hallowed be thy name;
thy kingdom come;
thy will be done;
on earth as it is in heaven.
Give us this day our daily bread.
And forgive us our trespasses,
as we forgive those who trespass against us.
And lead us not into temptation;
but deliver us from evil.
For thine is the kingdom,
the power, and the glory,
for ever and ever. Amen.**

14   THE CONCLUDING COLLECT

This or some other collect:

Heavenly Father,
who chose the Virgin Mary

to be the mother of our Lord and Saviour:
fill us with your grace,
that in all things we may accept your holy will
and with her rejoice in your salvation;
through Jesus Christ our Lord. **Amen.**

15 THE FINAL PRAYERS

The Lord be with you:
and also with you.

Let us bless the Lord.
Thanks be to God.

May the almighty God,
the Father, the Son, and the Holy Spirit,
guard us and give us his blessing.
Amen.

Appendix A

Scripture Sentences

One of the following may replace the sentence at Section 1 in the Office.

16 Mary said, 'Behold I am the handmaid of the Lord; let it be to me according to your word.' *Luke 1:38*

17 Shout for joy, daughter of Zion, Israel, shout aloud! Rejoice, exult with all your heart, daughter of Jerusalem! The Lord, the king of Israel, is in your midst. *Zephaniah 3:14 and 15*

18　I saw a vast throng, which no one could count, from all
　　races and tribes, nations and languages, standing before
　　the throne and the Lamb . . . And they shouted aloud:
　　'Victory to our God who sits on the throne, and to the
　　Lamb!'　　　　　　　　　　　　　　　*Revelation 7:9 and 10*

19　At various times in the past and in various different
　　ways, God spoke to our ancestors through the prophets;
　　but in our own time, the last days, he has spoken to us
　　through his Son.　　　　　　　　　　*Hebrews 1:1 and 2*

Appendix B

Lessons and Responsories

*One of the following may replace the Lesson and Responsory
at Section 10 in the Office.*

20　Christ Jesus, though he was in the form of God, did not
　　count equality with God a thing to be grasped, but
　　emptied himself, taking the form of a servant, and was
　　born in human likeness.　　　　　　*Philippians 2:6 and 7*

　　　You, Christ, are the King of glory,
　　　the eternal Son of the Father.
　　　You, Christ, are the King of glory,
　　　the eternal Son of the Father.

　　　When you took our flesh to set us free
　　　You humbly chose the Virgin's womb.
　　　You, Christ, are the King of glory,
　　　the eternal Son of the Father.

Glory to the Father, and to the Son,
and to the Holy Spirit:
You, Christ, are the King of glory,
the eternal Son of the Father.

21   The word was made flesh, he lived among us, and we
saw his glory, the glory that is his as the only Son of the
Father, full of grace and truth.   *John 1:14*

Blessed are you, Son of Mary;
born a child, you shared our humanity.
Blessed are you, Son of Mary;
born a child, you shared our humanity.

Day by day we bless you,
and we praise your name for ever.
Blessed are you, Son of Mary;
born a child, you shared our humanity.

Glory to the Father, and to the Son,
and to the Holy Spirit:
Blessed are you, Son of Mary;
born a child, you shared our humanity.

22   Near the cross of Jesus stood his mother and his
mother's sister, Mary the wife of Clopas, and Mary of
Magdala. Seeing his mother and the disciple he loved
standing near her, Jesus said to his mother, 'Woman,
this is your son.' Then to the disciple he said, 'This is
your mother.' And from that moment the disciple made
a place for her in his home.   *John 19:25–7*

We adore you, O Christ, and we bless you:
because by your holy cross
you have redeemed the world.
**We adore you, O Christ, and we bless you:
because by your holy cross
you have redeemed the world.**

Christ himself bore our sins in his body on the tree.
**We adore you, O Christ, and we bless you:
because by your holy cross
you have redeemed the world.**

Glory to the Father, and to the Son,
and to the Holy Spirit:
**We adore you, O Christ, and we bless you:
because by your holy cross
you have redeemed the world.**

23 Praise be to the God and Father of our Lord Jesus
Christ! In his great mercy, he has given us new birth
with a living hope by the resurrection of Jesus Christ
from the dead.   *1 Peter 1:3*

Christ has been raised from the dead,
the first fruits of those who have fallen asleep.
**Christ has been raised from the dead,
the first fruits of those who have fallen asleep.**

Thanks be to God, who gives us the victory
through our Lord Jesus Christ.
**Christ has been raised from the dead,
the first fruits of those who have fallen asleep.**

Glory to the Father, and to the Son,
and to the Holy Spirit. Alleluia! Alleluia!
Christ has been raised from the dead,
the first fruits of those who have fallen asleep.
Alleluia! Alleluia!

24   With one accord the apostles devoted themselves to
prayer, together with Mary the mother of Jesus, and his
brothers.   *Acts 1:14*

You send forth your Spirit, O Lord;
you renew the face of the earth.
You send forth your Spirit, O Lord;
you renew the face of the earth.

The love of God has been poured into our hearts
through the Holy Spirit.
You send forth your Spirit, O Lord;
you renew the face of the earth.

Glory to the Father, and to the Son,
and to the Holy Spirit:
You send forth your Spirit, O Lord;
you renew the face of the earth.

Appendix C

Concluding Collects

One of the following may replace the Concluding Collect at
Section 15 in the Office.

25 ANNUNCIATION

Pour your grace into our hearts, O Lord,
that as we have known the incarnation
of your Son, Jesus Christ,
by the message of an angel,
so by his cross and passion
we may be brought to the glory of his resurrection;
through Jesus Christ our Lord. **Amen.**

26 CONCEPTION

Almighty and everlasting God, who by the
overshadowing of the Holy Spirit prepared the body
and soul of the glorious Virgin-Mother Mary to be a
dwelling-place for your Son; grant that we who rejoice
in her commemoration may at her tender intercession
be kept unspotted, and made a pure temple for his
dwelling; who is alive and reigns with you and the same
Spirit, God for ever and ever. **Amen.**

27 VISITATION

Almighty God, who led the Blessed Virgin Mary to
visit Elizabeth to their great comfort and joy; grant
that, as Mary rejoiced to be called the mother of the
Lord, so we may always rejoice to believe in him as our
Saviour, both God and man, to whom with you and the
Holy Spirit be all honour and glory, now and for ever.
Amen.

28 INCARNATION

Almighty and everlasting God, you have stooped to
raise our fallen humanity by the child-bearing of
blessed Mary; grant that we who have seen your glory
revealed in our human nature, and your love made
perfect in our weakness, may daily be renewed in your
image, and conformed to the pattern of your Son, Jesus
Christ our Lord. **Amen.**

29   Most loving Father, who by the obedience of Mary did repair the sin of Eve; grant that we who venerate the Virgin Mother of the Lord may follow her in faithfulness, and at length attain the company of your saints in heaven; through Jesus Christ our Lord. **Amen.**

30   Almighty and everlasting God, the light of the faithful and the ruler of souls, as you have hallowed us by the incarnation of your Word, and the child-bearing of the Blessed Virgin Mary, let the power of your Holy Spirit come also upon us, and the mercy of the Most High overshadow us, for you live and reign with the Son, and the Holy Spirit, one God, for ever and ever. **Amen.**

31   O Christ our God incarnate, whose Virgin Mother was blessed in bearing you, but still more blessed in keeping your word; grant us, who honour the exaltation of her lowliness, to follow the example of her devotion to your will, for you live and reign with the Father and the Holy Spirit, God for ever and ever. **Amen.**

32   AT THE CROSS
O Lord Jesus Christ, Son of the living God, whose love, streaming from the bare Cross, entrusted your best beloved, mother and disciple, each to the other; bestow on us the grace and glory of forgetting ourselves in a constant tender healing of the sorrows of those whom you love; for your mercy's sake. **Amen.**

33   REPOSE OF THE BLESSED VIRGIN MARY
Almighty God, who received the Blessed Virgin Mary into your eternal presence; grant that, through the merits of your Son, our Saviour Jesus Christ, we may, with his glorious Mother, be crowned and pavilioned for ever, by your own immortal love, where you live and reign with the Son and the Holy Spirit, one God, world without end. **Amen.**

Appendix D

Devotional Texts

One of the following Prayers or Anthems may be said together at the close of the Office.

34 Salve, Regina, Mater misericordiae;
    vita, dulcedo, et spes nostra salve.
    Ad te clamamus, exsules filii Hevae,
    ad te suspiramus gementes et flentes
    in hac lacrimarum valle.
    Eia ergo advocata nostra, illos tuos
    misericordes oculos ad nos converte;
    Et Jesum, benedictum fructum ventris tui,
    nobis post hoc exilium ostende
    O clemens, O pia, O dulcis Virgo Maria.

35 Hail, holy Queen, mother of mercy;
    hail, our life, our sweetness, and our hope!
    To you do we cry, poor banished children of Eve;
    to you do we send up our sighs, mourning and weeping
    in this vale of tears.
    Turn then, most gracious advocate,
    your eyes of mercy towards us;
    and after this our exile,
    show to us the blessed fruit of your womb, Jesus.
    O clement, O loving, O Sweet Virgin Mary.

36 We greet you, holy Queen
    our life, our joy and hope.
    Mother full of mercy, we cry to you in trust.
    Exiled children of fallen Eve,
    see our sighs and tears,
    see our world of sadness.

Mother, plead for us.
Turn then towards us those eyes that plead our cause,
and when our life on earth is done,
show us then your Son,
blessed fruit of your virgin womb,
Jesus Christ our God.
O Mary, full of kindness,
O Mary, full of love,
O joyful Mary, full of peace and grace

Mount St Bernard's Abbey

37　O Lord, we praise and magnify your Name
For the Most Holy Virgin-Mother of God,
Who is the highest of your saints,
The most glorious of all your creatures,
The most perfect of all your works,
The nearest to you, in the throne of God,
Whom you were pleased to make
Daughter of the Eternal Father,
Mother of the Eternal Son,
Spouse of the Eternal Spirit,
Tabernacle of the most glorious Trinity.
Mother of Jesus,
Mother of the Messiah,
Mother of the Desire of Nations,
Mother of the Prince of Peace,
Mother of the King of Heaven,
Mother of our Creator,
Mother and Virgin,
Mirror of humility and obedience,
Mirror of wisdom and devotion,
Mirror of modesty and chastity,
Mirror of sweetness and resignation,
Mirror of sanctity,
Mirror of all virtues.　　　　*Thomas Traherne (1637–74)*

38   Almighty God, we offer you most high praise and
hearty thanks for the wonders of your grace and virtue,
which you have declared in all your saints, and which
you have bestowed on your holy church from the
beginning of the world; but chiefly in the glorious and
most blessed Virgin Mary, the Mother of your Son,
Jesus Christ our Lord; as also in the blessed Angels in
heaven and in all other holy persons who, in their lives
and labours, have shone forth as lights to the world in
their own generations.   *Bishop John Cosin*

39   LLANFAIR

> Joy to you, O Queen above, Alleluia!
> Sing the victory of love, Alleluia!
> God has raised the Son you bore, Alleluia!
> All your prayers we now implore, Alleluia!

40   Commemorating our most holy, most pure, most
blessed and glorious Lady, Mary ever Virgin and
Mother of God, with all the saints, let us commend
ourselves and one another and our whole life to Christ
our God; for to you, O Lord, belongs all glory, all
honour and all worship, now and for ever. **Amen.**
                     Liturgy of St John Chrysostom

41   Mary the Dawn, but Christ the perfect Day.
Mary the Gate, but Christ the heavenly Way.
Mary the Root, but Christ the mystic Vine.
Mary the Grape, but Christ the sacred Wine.
Mary the Corn-Sheaf, Christ the Living Bread.
Mary the Rose-Tree, Christ the Rose blood-red.
Mary the Fount, but Christ the cleansing Flood.
Mary the Chalice, Christ the saving Blood.

Mary the Beacon, Christ the haven's Rest.
Mary the Mirror, Christ the Vision blest.

Source unknown

42   Beneath the shelter of your tender compassion
we flee for refuge, Mother of God
Do not overlook my supplications in adversity,
but deliver us out of danger;
for you alone are chaste and blessed.

Earliest known invocation of Mary c 360 AD
Tr. John McHugh

43   Mary,
by love's sacrifice
your heart is pierced.
Mary,
by love's generosity
you are emptied.
Mary,
in temptation
may we imitate your obedience.
Mary,
in the hour of trial
may we know
the love you gazed upon
at Calvary.

based on Frank Topping An Impossible God

44   O Holy Spirit, Lord and Giver of life, as you
overshadowed Mary that she might be the Mother of
Jesus our Saviour, so work silently in my heart, to form
within me the fulness of his redeemed and redeeming
humanity. Give me his loving heart, to burn with love
for God and love for my neighbour; give me a share of
his joy and sorrow, his weakness and his strength, his
labour for the world's salvation. May Mary, blessed

159

among women, Mother of our Saviour, pray for me,
that Christ may be formed in me, that I may live in
union of heart and will with Jesus Christ, her Son, our
Lord and Saviour. **Amen.**   *Cheslyn Jones*

Sources and Acknowledgements

6 Words: © Mrs J. R. Peacey.
7 *The Psalms: A New Translation for Worship* © English Text 1976,
   1977 David L. Frost et al., (Collins Liturgical Psalter).
8 The Joint Liturgical Group: *The Daily Office Revised* SPCK, 1978.
9 Scripture quotations are from *The Revised Standard Version of the
   Bible* (1946, 1952, © 1971, 1973), *The Jerusalem Bible* © 1966
   Darton, Longman and Todd and Doubleday and Co Inc, and *The
   Revised English Bible* 1989 © Oxford University Press and Cambridge
   University Press.
10 International Consultation on English Texts (ICET).
11 Original to this compilation; Norman Wallwork 1981.
12 As 11.
14 The Joint Liturgical Group: *The Daily Office Revised* SPCK, 1978.
20 Responsory from English Language Liturgical Consultation version of
   the *Te Deum* 1989 ©.
21 Responsory (main refrain) from *The Book of Alternative Services* of
   the Anglican Church of Canada © 1985 The General Synod of the
   Anglican Church of Canada, 600 Jarvis Street, Toronto, Ontario,
   Canada M4Y 2J6 (Christmas and Epiphany Introductory Responses).
26 E. Milner-White *Cambridge Offices and Orisons* Mowbrays, 1921.
27 *Book of Common Prayer* Church of the Province of South Africa
   SPCK London and Johannesburg, 1954.
28 As 26.
29 As 26 but adapted for *New English Hymnal* 1986.
30 Mozarabic—William Bright *Ancient Collects.*
31 William Bright *Ancient Collects.*
32 E. Milner-White *Procession of Passion Prayers* SPCK, 1950.
33 As 26, adapted by Norman Wallwork.
36 Mount Saint Bernard's Priory.
37 Bodleian Library, Oxford MS Eng.th.e.51.
39 © Norman Wallwork.
40 Liturgy of St John Chrysostom.
41 Supplied by Ven. George B. Timms.
42 John Rylands Library papyrus, with permission of John McHugh.
43 Frank Topping *An Impossible God* Collins Fount, 1985, p. 39.
44 Cheslyn Jones adapted by Norman Wallwork.